# TERRORISM
## ALL THAT MATTERS

*To Debbie*

# TERRORISM

## Andrew Silke

ALL THAT MATTERS

ALL THAT MATTERS

First published in Great Britain in 2014 by Hodder & Stoughton. An Hachette UK company.

First published in US in 2014 by The McGraw-Hill Companies, Inc

This edition published 2014

*British Library Cataloguing in Publication Data:* a catalogue record for this title is available from the British Library.

Paperback ISBN 978 1 444 16331 5

eBook ISBN 978 1 444 16333 9

*Library of Congress Catalog Card Number:* on file

10 9 8 7 6 5 4 3 2 1

The publisher has used its best endeavours to ensure that any website addresses referred to in this book are correct and active at the time of going to press. However, the publisher and the author have no responsibility for the websites and can make no guarantee that a site will remain live or that the content will remain relevant, decent or appropriate.

The publisher has made every effort to mark as such all words which it believes to be trademarks. The publisher should also like to make it clear that the presence of a word in the book, whether marked or unmarked, in no way affects its legal status as a trademark.

Every reasonable effort has been made by the publisher to trace the copyright holders of material in this book. Any errors or omissions should be notified in writing to the publisher, who will endeavour to rectify the situation for any reprints and future editions.

Typeset by Cenveo® Publisher Services.

Printed and bound in Great Britain by CPI Group (UK) Ltd., Croydon, CR0 4YY.

Hodder & Stoughton policy is to use papers that are natural, renewable and recyclable products and made from wood grown in sustainable forests. The logging and manufacturing processes are expected to conform to the environmental regulations of the country of origin.

Hodder & Stoughton Ltd

338 Euston Road

London NW1 3BH

www.hodder.co.uk

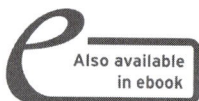

**Also available in ebook**

# Contents

# What *is* terrorism?

*All cruelty springs from weakness.*

*Seneca*

ALL THAT MATTERS

Eleven minutes after take-off, United Airlines flight 629 was rocked by an explosion. The aircraft, already several thousand feet above the ground, disintegrated in mid-air, killing all 44 people on board. Crash investigators initially suspect mechanical failure as the most likely cause, but FBI forensic analysis detects traces of explosives, and reveals that a bomb had been hidden in the suitcase of an unsuspecting passenger.

This, however, was not a terrorist attack. FBI agents quickly identify the bomber as 22-year-old John Gilbert Graham and the unsuspecting passenger who carried the bomb on board was his *mother*, killed minutes after signing a life insurance document in the airport hall. Her son, already a convicted fraudster, was named as the sole beneficiary and stood to receive $37,500. Graham's motive for the bombing was purely personal financial gain. That 44 people had to die for him to receive this pay-out was incidental as far as he was concerned. He certainly did not care about any wider political or social effects of the bombing.

Perhaps strangely, the FBI was not at all surprised by the direction the investigation had taken. Indeed, once it realized that a bomb was involved, the FBI focused almost all its attention on suspects who would benefit from insurance pay-outs. There was no serious consideration that political motives might have played a part in the attack. An odd perspective in today's world, but back in 1955, when Graham carried out this bombing, the world was a very different place. At that time, when passenger aircraft were attacked the motive was almost always insurance.

Things change. Contrast Graham's bombing with another attack against a passenger aircraft some 30 years later. In April 1986, another unsuspecting passenger was carrying in her luggage a bomb designed to explode when the flight was in mid-air. The passenger was a pregnant Irish woman, Ann-Marie Murphy, who was on her way to Israel to marry the father of her unborn child.

Ann-Marie had met the father, Jordanian-born Nesar Hindawi, while they were both working in London. A relationship ensued, and in November 1985, Ann-Marie discovered she was pregnant. Hindawi was abroad at the time and when Ann-Marie phoned him, he advised her to have an abortion. She refused and said she would raise the baby on her own. She believed the relationship was over, but then

> 'suddenly Nezar was at the door of my flat. He said we'd marry and everything would be alright. It was like a big weight had been lifted from me ... He was very tender and loving and told me of his plans to marry in the Holy Land.'

What Ann-Marie did not know, was that Hindawi was the leader of a tiny, Syrian-backed terrorist group, the Jordanian Revolutionary Movement. Hindawi provided Ann-Marie with the money for a wedding dress and paid for a flight to Tel Aviv on the Israeli airline El Al. He said work commitments meant that he would have to follow shortly afterwards. He also provided his pregnant girlfriend with a new suitcase. On 17 April 1986, Hindawi drove with Ann-Marie to Heathrow airport. In the taxi on the way to the airport, Hindawi took a calculator out of the suitcase and inserted a battery. This activated a bomb which was concealed in the case. Fortunately for the unsuspecting Irish woman (and the other 375 passengers on El Al flight 016), Ann-Marie's luggage was subjected to a routine security check. It was almost cleared, when a staff member became suspicious about the weight of the suitcase when its contents had been emptied. The bomb was discovered and Ann-Marie was detained. The authorities quickly realized that the poor woman had been duped by her boyfriend. Hindawi was arrested the next day, and was eventually sentenced to 45 years in prison.

Both plots were extremely callous, but the principal reason Hindawi's attempt is regarded as terrorism whereas Graham's is not, is *motive*. Hindawi was carrying out his attack to benefit a political cause, and it is the political element which is the defining feature of terrorism.

An act of terrorism is never just aimed at its direct victims but always has in mind other audiences. Graham had a narrow focus and was just concerned with killing his mother and receiving an insurance pay-out. The impact the bombing might have on others had no interest for him. Terrorists, in contrast, are very interested in the wider impact of their violence. In most cases, for them it is the wider impact which is the most important element. Usually there is no personal connection with the victims and the animosity felt towards those who are killed and injured is typically abstract. As an Italian terrorist said of the victims, 'we were not concerned with the elimination of a person but of what he represented'.

Bearing this in mind, there is still intensely fierce controversy over what is and is not an act of terrorism. As the judge who was asked to define pornography drily replied, 'I might not be able to define it for you, but I know it when I see it'. Terrorism falls into a similar camp. Indeed, many members of the general public are puzzled that governments and international organizations seem to have so much trouble agreeing a definition.

The failure to find a widely acceptable definition of terrorism is tied to the political use of the word. Terrorism is unquestionably politically motivated, but fundamentally 'terrorism' is also a pejorative word with a range of negative meanings. For this reason, many media organizations such as the BBC and Reuters are extremely reluctant to describe any individual or group in their reports as 'terrorists', preferring instead to use terms such as 'militants', 'insurgents' or 'guerrillas'. These concerns tie into the long-standing truism that 'one man's terrorist, is another man's freedom fighter'. Individuals such as Nelson Mandela, for example, were labelled as terrorists for many years, and yet Mandela went on to become an internationally respected statesman. (Indeed, it is worth noting that the terrorists eventually win the conflict in up to 10 per cent of cases.)

A further thorny issue hangs over the question of whether states themselves can be terrorists. States certainly commit acts of violence, and state violence is routinely far more lethal and destructive than the violence carried out by non-state actors. In the 20th century, wars killed an estimated 231 million people and the biggest death tolls usually occurred when fully fledged states slugged it out with each other. Up to 15 million people were killed in the First World War. That slaughter was dwarfed by the Second World War, which resulted in as many as 75 million deaths. Civil wars fought between governments and their opponents account for a hefty proportion of the remaining deaths, with the Chinese civil war alone, for example, resulting in 6.2 million deaths between 1946 and 1950.

Formidable losses also occurred when states turned their power towards repressing elements of their own population, usually in an effort to utterly crush dissent. Internal repression in the Soviet Union between 1920 and 1956 resulted in at least 35 million deaths, considerably more than the USSR suffered in its titanic struggle with Germany in the Second World War. Even this figure pales compared with the number killed within China between 1950 and 1976, as government policies resulted in even greater suffering and led to the deaths of nearly 47 million people (many through starvation).

Where, then, does terrorism lie in such contexts? Terrorism is often seen as belonging particularly to the messier conflicts of the past century, the small wars, revolutions and insurgencies which often defy neat classification. What the difference might be between a rebel, an insurgent and a terrorist is not clear, beyond perhaps a tacit acknowledgement from a government that when you use a label like 'insurgent', the enemy is probably a more serious threat and is possibly heading towards (or might already be in) a sufficiently strong position to be worth negotiating with.

Conflicts in this muddled category include, for example, the violence in Sri Lanka between the Tamil Tigers (LTTE) and the Sri Lankan government. Between 1980 and 2009 this conflict caused nearly 80,000 deaths, most of them inevitably of civilians. Despite the scale of the violence, the Sri Lankan government largely succeeded in having the LTTE regarded as a terrorist organization by the international community, rather than as a rival in a bitter civil war; and this despite the fact that the LTTE for many years was strong enough to control significant parts of the country.

Similar propaganda success was eventually achieved by Russia in its battle with Chechen separatists. Between 1994 and 2000, some 113,500 people were killed – most of them Chechen civilians – as the region attempted to break away from the Russian Federation. Initially the West proved reluctant to view the Chechens as simply another group of terrorists, and more often than not criticized the heavy-handed Russian approach to the conflict. That largely changed after 9/11, in the wake of alleged links between the Chechens and Al-Qaeda, and the Chechens' undeniable use of suicide bombers and mass casualty attacks against civilian targets.

Yet for some, terrorism is as much about the internal repression carried out by states as it is about violence emanating from sub-state movements. Without question, there is wide acceptance that the word 'terrorism' originally emerged to describe exactly such violence. The expression appeared in the 18th century when the government of Revolutionary France butchered up to 40,000 French citizens as part of a 'Reign of Terror' as it sought to crush internal dissent. The chief architect of the slaughter, Maximilien Robespierre, summed up its purpose succinctly:

> 'We must smother the internal and external enemies of the Republic or perish with it; now in this situation, the first maxim of your policy ought to be to lead the people by reason and the people's enemies by terror.'

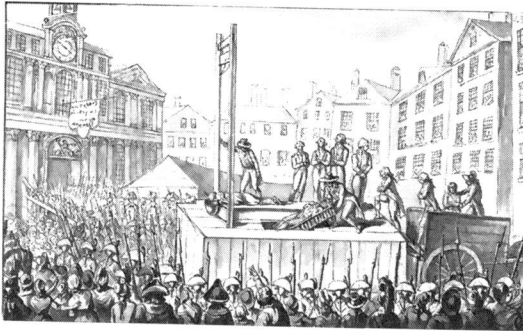

▲ The birth of terrorism: the French Revolution's 'Reign of Terror'.

The common usage of the term 'terrorism', however, drifted away from its early origins. As often happens in living languages, the original meaning of a word can be watered down and then largely lost, replaced by more contemporary connotations. This has certainly happened with regard to 'terrorism' which, while originally applied to something that governments did, has now in the wider consciousness become increasingly viewed as primarily something that non-state actors do. This shift to non-state actors happened early, and by 1868, for example, many American newspapers routinely described the violence carried out by the newly emerged Ku Klux Klan as 'terrorism'. This change towards seeing terrorism as something non-state groups did gathered pace, and by the end of the 20th century among the wider public the word was used almost exclusively within that context.

Even accepting a general trend towards seeing terrorism as something that non-state actors do, however, does not let governments entirely off the hook. Many states have unquestionably sponsored terrorist groups in different parts of the world. In the 1980s, for example, Libya secretly shipped an estimated 130 tonnes of weapons and munitions to the Provisional IRA. This haul included at least 5 tonnes of Semtex-H explosive, which became a key ingredient in IRA bombs in the following years. Such a massive injection of weaponry virtually guaranteed that the IRA would have the means to continue their terrorist campaign for decades to come if they wished (and some of the Libyan munitions have fallen under the control of dissident republican groups today, though the aging Semtex has lost much of its potency). Libya did not really care about the IRA's ultimate aim of a united Ireland, but fully realized that the IRA's violence would prove troublesome for the UK government. Indeed, the Libyans demonstrated their utter indifference to the politics of Northern Ireland by also supplying loyalist paramilitaries with weapons – weapons which would be used by the loyalists to try to kill *IRA members and their supporters*. Having supplied two sides of the conflict with weapons, the Libyans were content to sit back and watch sparks fly, knowing that the ultimate cost of the conflict would have to be borne by the British government, the real target of Libyan ire.

Overall, many states have found terrorist groups are a highly effective way to wage a proxy war against powerful enemies. In the Middle East, both Syria and Iran have invested heavily in sponsoring the Lebanese-based group Hezbollah. In return for substantial funds, weapons and training, Iran and Syria have both been able to prod Hezbollah into attacking Israel. Israel is too formidable for either country to seriously consider attacking it directly, but Hezbollah gives both states a useful proxy to harass Israel at low risk to themselves, knowing that major Israeli retaliation for any attacks will usually focus on the Lebanese militant group.

States too also continue to engage in types of violence which, if it had been committed by a non-state group, would widely be seen as terrorism. Perhaps one of the best examples of this occurred in June 1985, when the Greenpeace ship *Rainbow Warrior* was bombed by French secret service agents as it lay in harbour in New Zealand. The ship was attacked in order to stop it interfering with nuclear tests the French were planning in the South Pacific and one crew member was killed in the explosion. Two French agents were captured by the New Zealand authorities, though others escaped. The two who were captured were convicted of the bombing but were released after serving less than two years in prison.

The case bears comparison with the murder of Ahmed Bouchiki in July 1973 in Norway. Bouchiki was an innocent Moroccan-born waiter living in Lillehammer, Norway. Israeli intelligence, however, mistakenly believed that he was Ali Hassan Salameh, a senior PLO official and the leader of Force 17, Yasser Arafat's personal bodyguard. Significantly, the Israelis believed that Salameh had been involved in planning the Black September attack against Israeli athletes at the Munich Olympics. In retaliation for the Munich massacre, an Israeli assassination team was dispatched to Norway to eliminate 'Salameh'. After the unfortunate Bouchiki was shot dead by the hit team, members of the Israeli squad were captured by the Norwegian police before they could flee the country, although the two actual shooters managed to escape to Israel. Five were convicted of their involvement in Bouchiki's murder, but they received very light prison sentences given the circumstances, and all were released from custody within two years.

A more recent and on-going campaign concerns scientists working as part of Iran's nuclear industry. Amid fears that Iran is actively trying to develop nuclear weapons, a number of her scientists have been killed in a series of high-profile attacks. These assassinations are almost certainly the work of a foreign government, with Israel being the most likely culprit. In November 2010 Majid Shahriari, who was based in the nuclear engineering department of Tehran's Shahid Beheshti University, was killed when motorcyclists drove alongside his car and attached a magnetized bomb. Further killings have followed. The attacks are clearly designed to undermine Iran's nuclear programme, not only through the direct loss of the scientists who are killed and seriously injured, but also through the impact the killings have on Iran's wider scientific community. Surviving experts know they are under serious threat if they continue working within the nuclear programme. The campaign then represents classic terrorism: not only are people killed but a stark message is sent to a much wider audience. This, then, is the terror that Robespierre found so useful and in it we perhaps have a genuine key to unlocking what terrorism actually is.

Ultimately the purest essence of terrorism is violence. This violence is carried out in order to compel an enemy to do the will of the terrorists. Running through its heart there is always a political agenda. Politics here encompasses how society runs and works at a range of levels from the social to the economic to the religious. The terrorist is using force – and the threat of further violence – to dictate how these worlds operate. It is an intensely psychological act of aggression. The aim is not to kill or maim everyone. The aim rather is to kill some – and sometimes very few indeed – but more importantly to terrify the remainder into complying with the terrorist's will.

# 2

# A brief history of terrorism

*Kill one, frighten ten thousand.*

*Ancient Chinese saying*

ALL THAT
MATTERS

The history of terrorism stretches back over two thousand years and arguably much longer. Despite such a legacy, there has been a repeated tendency to view terrorism as an exclusively modern phenomenon, with each generation failing to see the earlier incarnations or, if they do perceive them, being quick to dismiss it all as completely unlike the terrorism we have today. The 9/11 attacks exacerbated this problem and academic studies looking at the history of terrorism declined significantly in the decade after 2001, while research on almost every other aspect of terrorism increased hugely. There was an implicit message in this trend: the past has nothing to teach us about terrorism. This is a new age and we face a new threat, the lessons of former days no longer apply.

Having dispensed with any need to pay attention to the warnings of history, governments rapidly committed a series of blunders in the 'war on terror' which for a considerable period of time simply made Al-Qaeda and its affiliates stronger and more popular. While there has been some belated recognition of these errors, even now, more than a decade on, the damage has still not been entirely undone and the war on terror itself shows no sign of ending. Had there been even slightly more awareness of the history of terrorism, a great many mistakes could have been avoided. Nothing Al-Qaeda has done over the past 20 years is unique. On the contrary, everything from their religious ideology to co-ordinated suicide attacks to using planes as flying bombs has been done by others before.

This volume is too slim for a detailed examination of the history of terrorism, but to pull out some key lessons we will look at two historical groups, one from 150 years ago and the other from nearly 2,000 years ago. Both show surprising parallels with modern terrorist groups, and both have important lessons to teach those who are willing to see them. As T. E. Lawrence – one of the most gifted insurgent leaders of the 20th century – warned, 'with 2,000 years of examples behind us we have no excuse when fighting, for not fighting well.' We ignore the history of terrorism at our peril.

# ▶ The Sicarii

In 6 AD, Judea was annexed by the Roman Empire. The occupation led to the development of a series of revolutionary Messianic movements, and the widespread belief that a Messiah would soon come to liberate the Jewish people. Some felt that the ground needed to be prepared for the arrival of this Messiah and such preparations took the form of igniting conflict with the Romans. One of the most important of these groups was the Sicarii. The Sicarii gained their name from a short dagger – the *sica* – that they carried hidden in their cloaks. A favourite tactic was to mingle with crowds during a festival or market day and launch a surprise attack on an unsuspecting target. As the victim collapsed with multiple stab wounds, the attackers would melt back into the crowds, concealing their daggers under their cloaks. Their ultimate aim was to free the Jewish people from Roman rule, and to do this they were not only willing to target Romans but also any Jews who assisted the Romans. This was clear from one of the very first attacks attributed to the group when, in 54 AD, they murdered a high priest in Jerusalem because he was deemed to be too pro-Roman. Over the next ten years, violence by the group and linked bands steadily increased. While the main purpose was to end Roman rule, most of those killed in the group's attacks were actually locals. The organization targeted members of the local administration, Jewish women who fraternized with Romans, Jews who worked for the Romans, Jewish shopkeepers or merchants who sold produce to the Romans, in short anyone who in any way could be seen as supporting the occupation.

The key source for information on the Sicarii is Flavius Josephus, a Jewish historian who, though not a member of the Sicarii, lived during the conflict and initially fought against the Romans. Reliance on his account must be tempered, however, by the fact that he switched sides later in the conflict and ended up fighting for the Romans. Written in the aftermath of what was ultimately a Roman victory, his history is generally pro-Roman in outlook, albeit with an unusual degree of insight into who their opponents were and what motivated them.

Indications of a pro-Roman perspective can be seen in how Josephus generally describes the Sicarii. Most frequently he refers to them as a band of 'robbers'. Less frequently he refers to them as 'innovators', highlighting nicely the group's desire for change. His terminology in general resonates with official dispatches in the modern era, when terrorists are usually described as 'bandits' or some other type of criminal.

The success of the Sicarii campaign was based on two factors. First, a highly effective campaign of intimidation and assassination carried out against locals who either supported the Romans or advocated a conciliatory policy towards Roman rule. By killing the most vocal supporters and silencing the moderates, the Sicarii cleared the public space for their cause. This created the impression that the extremists were much more popularly supported than probably was really the case, a perception which grew until it gave birth to the reality.

A second crucial factor was the reaction of the Roman authorities to the growing threat. Josephus singles out the Roman governor Gessius Florus as a major cause of the terrorists' success. As disturbances grew in the region, Florus ordered increasingly punitive measures to be taken in response to the violence. Arrogant, rude, high-handed and avaricious, Florus lacked what it took to win a local battle for hearts and minds. It did not help either that Roman intelligence on who the extremists were was poor, and the crackdown targeted a high proportion of innocents. The measures taken ranged from deliberate snubs to the Jewish populace and local leaders, the confiscation of property, the rounding up, torture and crucifixion of suspected troublemakers (many, if not most, of whom Josephus claims were innocent), to finally using the military to violently disperse crowds and carry out local massacres. These tactics played right into the hands of the extremists, increasing the support and sympathy they enjoyed, while alienating local communities from the Roman authorities. Indeed, the tactics were so counter-productive that Josephus suggested that Florus must have secretly *wanted* a full-scale rebellion to erupt. In hindsight, it was probably convenient to blame what happened on a bad governor, but an equally plausible explanation is that Florus genuinely wanted to defeat the terrorists and, like many rulers after him, he came to believe that increasingly aggressive and harsh measures were the best way to achieve this. That strategy, however, failed him spectacularly.

Florus, though, had certainly not been helped by his predecessors. Roman governors were notorious for viewing their position as primarily an excellent opportunity to wring what bribes and lucre they could from a foreign posting, and the previous governor in Judea, Albinus, was no exception. Albinus seems to have been particularly inept and outrageously corrupt. When he first arrived, he instituted a crackdown against the Sicarii but this waned after about a year, following which he invested little effort in controlling or subduing them. On the contrary, as time progressed he allowed imprisoned extremists to buy their freedom if they could raise enough money – a policy which enriched Albinus' personal purse but paved the way for many captured leaders to return to the field. He also released prisoners as part of hostage exchanges. Albinus enjoyed a good working relationship with the High Priest Ananias, and when the High Priest's son was kidnapped by the Sicarii, Albinus agreed to release ten named prisoners in return for his safe release. Not surprisingly, having succeeded with this exchange, the Sicarii then embarked on a sustained campaign of kidnappings to facilitate the release of even more of their comrades.

As well as allowing a growing number of prisoner releases, Albinus was also alleged to have accepted substantial bribes to turn a blind eye to the extremists' activities. It is no surprise that Florus inherited a dangerously unstable situation when he arrived. His heavy hand saw an end to corrupt practices but he swung the pendulum wildly in a more extreme direction.

And yet, why did the extremists think they could win in the first place? After all, the Roman Empire was by far the most formidable power of the age in Europe and the Near East. In a compelling speech shortly before the full rebellion erupted, the Jewish King Agrippa tried to warn the extremists to think about what they were attempting:

> 'What sort of an army do you rely on? What are the arms you depend on? Where is your fleet, that may seize upon the Roman seas? And where are those treasures which may be sufficient for your undertakings? ... Will you not carefully reflect upon the Roman Empire? Will you not estimate your own weakness? Hath not your army been often beaten even by your neighbouring nations, while the power of the Romans is invincible in all parts of the habitable earth? ... What therefore do you pretend to? Are you richer than the Gauls, stronger than the Germans, wiser than the Greeks, more numerous than all men upon the habitable earth? What confidence is it that elevates you to oppose the Romans?'

The warning fell on deaf ears. Elsewhere, Josephus says that he too tried to convince some of the militants that a confrontation with Rome could only end in disaster:

'But I could not persuade them; for the madness of desperate men was quite too hard for me.' He ceased his criticism out of fear he would be seen as too pro-Roman and seized and killed by the terrorists: 'I knew the power of the Romans was superior to all others, but did not say so [publicly] because of the robbers.'

The virulent campaign of assassination and intimidation provoked the desired response. A mass revolt against the Romans eventually erupted in 66 AD, shortly after the Sicarii seized the fortress of Masada to the south of Jerusalem. Florus attempted to restore order with local forces but was badly beaten. A full legion was rushed from neighbouring Syria but although it briefly reached the walls of Jerusalem, it was forced to retreat, suffering very heavy losses and losing its eagle in the process. By early 67 AD Jerusalem was a free city.

The Sicarii had achieved a classic terrorist victory. What began as a limited campaign of assassination and intimidation eventually provoked a widespread rebellion (courtesy of inept responses by the authorities). In general terms, this is exactly the same goal most modern terrorist groups hope to achieve. The Sicarii, however, would squander their new-found freedom. As often happens in the aftermath of revolution, the revolutionaries turned on themselves. The Romans had barely departed before a vicious power struggle erupted and the tactics which had been used against the Romans and their supporters were now turned on each other. Jerusalem, literally, became a divided city, with three factions seizing control of different districts. For three years they squabbled and fought amongst each other. Jerusalem did not stay free.

After the repulse of the Syrian legion, the Romans organized a far stronger force to retake Judea. Eight legions were dispatched – committing well over a quarter of the entire manpower of the Roman military. For three years the Romans steadily ground down Jewish resistance until, in 70 AD, a powerful Roman army finally reached the walls of Jerusalem and placed the city under siege. Incredibly, the factions inside the city had continued to bicker and attack each other and only stopped when Roman soldiers could finally be seen from the walls. It was too late. After a bitter siege lasting 134 days Jerusalem was sacked, and the rebels routed. Fighting continued in the region for a further three years, and did not stop until the final Sicarii stronghold at Masada was captured in 73 AD. In an act of final defiance, the Sicarii and their families committed mass suicide rather than be captured and taken into slavery by the Romans.

# ▶ The will of the people

Attempts were made in 1873 by some 2,500 young but highly educated Russians to incite the country's peasantry to revolt. The students moved out into the countryside and the villages, dressed like the peasants and tried to teach them the gospel of self-help through revolution. While they were certainly downtrodden – and a great many enjoyed an existence little better than slavery – the peasants were distinctly unimpressed by the young students and their ideals. In many places the students found themselves the target of jeering and abuse. In some districts they were attacked and their activities reported to the authorities. Thousands were arrested and the plan collapsed.

The peasant masses could not be simply *talked* into revolution. 'As long as the peasant has to work as he does to get himself a crust of bread,' one of the terrorist leaders concluded, 'you will never turn him into a political animal. ... They are practical men. They refuse to risk all for a will o' the wisp.' The student movement fractured in the aftermath of the debacle, with hard-liners coalescing around a new smaller group called *Narodnaya Volya* ('Will of the People'). This splinter faction came to the conclusion that more extreme measures were called for. If the masses could not be cajoled into an uprising, then it was up to the revolutionaries themselves to fight and defeat the government.

The first instances of violence occurred more or less spontaneously, sometimes as a reaction against brutal police officials. One of the most famous cases involved the shooting in St Petersburg of Governor-General Trepov by a young woman named Vera Zasulich. Trepov had lost his temper with an imprisoned student and – illegally – ordered him flogged almost to death. Vera Zasulich determined to kill Trepov in retaliation. In order to do so, she simply queued to speak with Trepov at a public meeting. When her turn finally came to speak with the General, the young woman pulled out a gun and shot him at point-blank range. He survived the injury, and Vera was instantly seized and brought to trial for attempted murder. However, so unpopular was Trepov that the jury, sensationally, found her not guilty and she was released and subsequently spirited out of Russia by sympathizers.

Vera's acquittal despite the clear-cut evidence against her was a severe warning to the authorities that the population was turning against them. The middle classes especially were increasingly sympathetic to the student movement and ever more aggrieved with the authoritarian nature of the State.

Though some tried to paint the Trepov shooting as the act of an isolated woman, in reality Vera had not acted alone. Simultaneous to her attempt to kill Trepov, a friend had tried – unsuccessfully – to kill another state official, and members of Narodnaya Volya had known about both plans and assisted with the preparations. Believing that Vera's example showed the way forward, the group now embarked on a full-scale campaign of terrorist attacks against the tsarist regime. As their leader argued: 'History moves too slowly. It needs a push.'

The group believed that because power in the Russian state was so highly centralized, the assassination of a few key individuals could cause the entire regime to collapse. Initially the campaign of violence focused on senior figures within the state's administration and a number of people were killed. Increasingly, however, the group came to believe that in order to effect serious change they would have to remove the tsar himself, Alexander II. With that decision, the group embarked on a breath-taking series of attempts to kill the Russian monarch.

One daring plot after another was launched against him. When he made a tour to Vladivostok using the newly completed trans-Siberian railway the terrorists attempted to blow up his train at three separate locations. He survived. The terrorists next tried to kill him in his own palace. In a plot that bore more than a passing resemblance to Guy Fawkes's audacious attempt to blow up the British Houses of Parliament in 1605, a workman, Stepan Khalturin, smuggled explosives into the palace and secreted them two floors beneath the tsar's private dining room. The police, however, gained intelligence that the terrorists had infiltrated the palace and security was massively increased. Hard-working and apparently reliable, Khalturin also played the country bumpkin and was popular with staff and guards. He worried, though, that the net was tightening around him. He asked a friendly guard how could one recognize a terrorist? It was easy, the guard replied. Terrorists were desperate-looking fellows with wild eyes and ferocious gestures. It was simple to spot them.

On 5 February 1880, the bomb was ready. It was set to detonate at a time when the tsar would normally take his dinner. Fate intervened. Alexander was delayed by a visiting dignitary and when the bomb exploded he was not in the room. Eleven people were killed and more than 50 injured.

The tsar's supporters claimed the repeated failures were proof that God was with Alexander and was shielding his life. The tsar himself did not place his fate entirely in the hands of the Almighty, and looked increasingly to his very capable minister of the interior, Count Loris-Melikov, to resolve the terrorist problem. Loris-Melikov was the best of Alexander's senior ministers and an excellent choice to tackle the terrorist threat. A successful general, Loris-Melikov combined intelligence with personal courage. He was also a political moderate who favoured reform. He advocated a two-pronged strategy. First, a co-ordinated security crackdown targeting the extremists and their supporters. This was to be an intelligence-led operation with more effort and resources devoted to identifying and tracking down the right people, especially the leaders who comprised the group's 'Executive Committee'. Second, a serious effort would be made to tackle some of the root causes of the violence. A process of reform which would at least start to address many of the genuine grievances of the Russian population was launched, including a move to introduce some democratic elements to the Russian system. Alexander baulked at some of the proposals, though over time he was gradually convinced to accept a growing number. The proposed reforms still lagged far behind what was then current in most Western countries (particularly in France, Great Britain and the USA) but nonetheless represented real progress by Russian standards.

The dual approach quickly started to bring benefits. The crackdown badly weakened the terrorist movement as key leaders were caught and imprisoned. The reform process also undermined wider support and sympathy for the on-going violence, especially among the middle classes. The terrorists found that they were fast losing existing members and were unable to recruit fresh blood. Even so, their commitment to assassinating

ALL THAT MATTERS: TERRORISM

the tsar remained. If he could just be eliminated, they believed, the situation could still be rescued. A final desperate effort was made to kill him.

In another remarkable plot, the group purchased a cheese shop close to the Winter Palace in St Petersburg, on a road the tsar was known to use regularly. They painstakingly dug a mine in the basement of the shop, which ran underneath the road outside. Once completed, the mine was filled with explosives ready to be detonated when the tsar's carriage passed above.

At the same time, a four-strong team were trained to use small bombs in case the mine failed. These bombs were essentially crude 5 lb grenades that were almost as dangerous to the bomb-throwers as to intended targets. The team were told they would have to be almost within touching distance of the tsar's carriage before they could throw the devices. Just two days before the planned attack, disaster struck when the group's leader, Andrei Zhelyabov, was arrested. Zhelyabov was heavily involved in the planning for the attack and knew all the details. He confirmed his identify to the police but revealed nothing about the plot.

On the day of the attack the tsar did not travel down the road of the cheese shop. The four bomb throwers moved to the street he would use. While they waited, the first bomb-thrower lost his nerve and fled. The second bomber kept his resolve and hurled his device at the tsar's carriage as it approached. The bomb exploded, fatally injuring a guard and a young boy, but did relatively little damage to the metal-lined carriage. Despite protests that he should continue on, the tsar stopped to inspect what had happened. The bomber had been seized and Alexander approached to question the young man. As he did so, a third bomber hurled his device. It exploded, killing the bomber instantly and seriously injuring Alexander, who died a few hours later.

▲ The assassination of Tsar Alexander II.

Killing the tsar was the high point for Narodnaya Volya but the movement had already entered its own death throes. Almost all of the executive committee had been captured before the attack. The surviving 19-year-old bomb-thrower now in police custody rapidly caved in to his interrogators, supplying details on the remaining members and their safe houses. Within eight days almost all of the most significant members had been captured, and within a month they were convicted and hanged.

Remnants of the terrorist group lingered for a while more. The following year they made an attempt to kill the new tsar, but it failed and eventually the survivors were crushed.

At the time it seemed that the terrorists had failed. The spectacular death of Alexander had not brought about the collapse of the regime. What it had destroyed was the reform process which had begun under Alexander's reign. Alexander had been a reluctant reformer at best, but his son was a total autocrat and Loris-Melikov's reforms were rapidly picked apart and undone. The clock was wound firmly back and Loris-Melikov himself was out of office within a year of the new tsar coming to power. The death of the reform process – more than the death of Alexander – was the lasting legacy of the terrorists. The lack of reform accelerated Russia's growing social, economic and political problems and Narodnaya Volya would provide a potent example to future Russian extremists of an appropriate answer to the country's deepening malaise.

In microcosm, both the Sicarii and Narodnaya Volya remain classic examples of terrorism. The Sicarii were motivated by ethnic, religious and nationalistic agendas, fighting for independence from an occupying foreign power. Narodnaya Volya were idealists fighting not for independence but to reform the existing system of government and to replace it with one of their own design. Almost all modern terrorists fall into one or other of these camps, and some, such as Al-Qaeda, have elements of both.

# 3

## Terrorist strategy and tactics

*We must spread our principles, not with words but with deeds, for this is the most popular, the most potent, and the most irresistible form of propaganda.*

*Mikhail Bakunin*

ALL THAT MATTERS

Terrorist violence is often portrayed as mindless and indiscriminate, but in reality terrorist attacks are usually the result of deliberate and considered planning, and the weighing up of different choices and options. Some terrorist attacks take years to plan. Others only days, or even hours. The tactics themselves are always intended to fit within a broader strategy, though the focus of that strategy can change as a campaign unfolds. Successful terrorist campaigns – from the perpetrators' perspective - can be broken down into four general elements:

▶ **Provocation** – the terrorists carry out acts of violence which are intended to provoke a strong reaction from the state and its forces. Normally one of the first reactions is to suspend or sideline the normal methods and operation of law and order. As the violence continues, there is an increasing role for the military, and special rules and regulations (often classed as 'emergency powers') are brought into the play. The terrorists are still referred to as criminals but they are no longer targeted or treated as criminals normally are.

▶ **Escalation** – having already convinced the state to abandon the old (and accepted) rule book, the terrorists attempt to increase the severity of attacks. This results in a demand for even greater security and protection. In response, the state takes increasingly severe and exceptional measures – sometimes including blatantly illegal tactics – in the search for victory.

▶ **Blame** – in the face of increased atrocities and rule-breaking on both sides, the conflict enters a blame phase where all parties attempt to place the responsibility for *all* atrocities at the door of the other. This is the classic battle for hearts and minds.

▶ **Endurance** – the final phase. The terrorists aim to break the will and morale of the state to sustain the conflict. Amid the carnage of the escalating violence and the battle for hearts and minds, the terrorists seek to convince the state and its supporters that the terrorists' commitment to the conflict and ability to stay in the fight is greater than the state's ability to continue to pay the mounting costs for the struggle. As belief in outright victory fades, the search for ways out and alternative solutions increases.

Fundamentally, terrorist conflicts are about breaking the will of the enemy. The terrorists are targeting the state's (and its supporters') belief that victory is possible or that the cost of the conflict can be borne any further. To do this, one does not need to kill all of the enemy's personnel or destroy all of its resources. One simply has to destroy the *idea* that ultimate victory is possible. Victory or defeat, then, ultimately boils down to a question of psychology.

A key difference between a terrorist conflict and a conventional military conflict is that the outcome depends far less on battlefield strength. Al-Qaeda, for example, is vastly weaker in military terms than the Iraqi military under Saddam Hussein's regime. Yet it took the Americans and their allies just 26 days to crush Saddam's army utterly in 2003. In contrast, the Americans have been chasing and fighting Al-Qaeda for well over 15 years, and by some estimates have already spent over $5 trillion on the struggle to destroy the movement and its allies. It is something of a shock to realize that, in real terms, this is more than the US spent fighting the Second World War (and if a few of the higher estimates are right, it is even more than the US spent fighting the two world wars and the Korean War combined). And still the end is not in sight.

This is the genius of terrorism. It offers an incredibly weak opponent the chance to inflict huge costs on a much larger and much more powerful foe.

## ▶ Hard and soft support

In order to successfully do this, however, terrorist groups need to reach a critical mass. A group needs to be able to:

▶ raise funds

▶ recruit

▶ replace the losses it will inevitably suffer in the slugging contest with the state.

Thus a crucial factor for any terrorist movement is its ability to mobilize support. Terrorist groups which fail to mobilize a support base can never be more than an irritant. Terrorist groups which succeed can become a strategic threat to the survival of a government.

Support for terrorist groups can essentially be broken down into *soft* support and *hard* support. Soft support, in practical terms, can be described as tolerance. Soft supporters of a terrorist group will not necessarily publicly voice their approval of the terrorist group's actions or aims, and they may not provide obvious tangible assistance to the group (e.g. in terms of financial contributions), neither would they necessarily vote for politicians connected with the terrorist group. However, the value of soft supporters is that they tend not to be willing to co-operate with the security forces in their efforts to police and apprehend the terrorists. They won't inform the security forces about the whereabouts or activities of members of the group, or alert the authorities if they see suspicious activity in their neighbourhood. Such support is tacit and often even unintentional – 'looking the other way' may simply be seen as the easier or safer option. Yet large numbers of soft supporters can be extremely valuable to terrorists, providing a community in which the terrorists can operate without much fear that the security and intelligence agencies will be made aware of what is happening.

Hard supporters represent an increased level of commitment. Hard supporters *will* try to provide the terrorists with practical assistance. At a political level they will vote for terrorist candidates in elections and they will be prepared to take part in demonstrations and protests on behalf of causes linked to the terrorists' aims. They will contribute financially to the terrorist group by making donations, buying merchandise or perhaps subscribing to publications produced by the terrorists. More committed supporters will also be prepared to store and hide weapons and other contraband for the group and may also be willing to provide safe houses for terrorists who are on the run or who are on 'active duty'. Hard supporters will also pass on intelligence about the security forces, possible targets or suspected informers to the terrorist group. While they may be a step away from being active terrorists, hard supporters are still integral to the effective running of any terrorist campaign.

For the terrorists, there is a relentless need to turn active non-supporters into soft supporters; and then to turn soft supporters into hard supporters. Examples of how this might be achieved include starting a campaign to improve the prison conditions for captured terrorists or by highlighting genuine human rights abuses committed by the government. Such campaigns can work to create the impression that the terrorists are more widely supported than is actually the case, and can also undermine the perceived legitimacy of the government.

In their instruction manuals for members, terrorist groups often focus on these issues at length, recognizing their crucial importance for the success of the movement. Consider this quote from IRA's instruction manual, the *Green Book*:

> *'Resistance must be channelled into active and passive support with an on-going process through our actions, our educational programmes, our policies, of attempting to turn the passive supporter into a dump holder, a member of the movement, a paper-seller, etc., with the purpose of building protective support barriers between the enemy and ourselves, thus curbing the enemy's attempted*

*isolation policy. And of course the more barriers there are, the harder it is for the enemy to get at us while at the same time we increase the potential for active support in its various forms.'*

# ▶ Ideology

Ideology sets the wider context for terrorist groups. It establishes who the enemy is and what the organization is fighting to achieve. Terrorist conflicts can be motivated by religious beliefs, nationalist and ethnic identities, and a wide range of political doctrines. In order to gain insight into a group's ideology, a good starting place is to examine the writings and publications of the movement. With regard to Al-Qaeda, for example, the writings of its current commander, Ayman al-Zawahiri, are highly informative:

> *'The first front is to inflict losses on the western crusader, especially to its economic infrastructure with strikes that would make it bleed for years. The strikes on New York, Washington, Madrid and London are the best examples for that. ... In the second front, we have to get crusaders out of the lands of Islam especially from Iraq, Afghanistan and Palestine. ... The third front is working at changing the corrupt regimes [in our countries], which have sold their honour to the Crusading West and befriended Israel. ... The fourth front is popularizing the Dawah [inviting non-Muslims to accept the truth of Islam] work.'*

This statement is very explicit in terms of the aims and objectives of the organization and also provides a candid insight into the types of targets the group is interested in (and why). Elsewhere in his writings, al-Zawahiri talks explicitly about the type of tactics Al-Qaeda and its affiliates should favour:

> '[We] need to inflict the maximum casualties against the opponent, for this is the language understood by the west, no matter how much time and effort such operations take.

> '[We] need to concentrate on the method of martyrdom operations as the most successful way of inflicting damage against the opponent and the least costly to the mujahideen in terms of casualties.

> 'The targets as well as the type and method of weapons used must be chosen to have an impact on the structure of the enemy and deter it.'

Having established an appropriate range of targets for violence, these manuals and other writings often go on to provide instructions on how to plan, prepare for and then carry out attacks (e.g. giving instructions on how to construct weapons and carry out reconnaissance of potential targets).

The general process for preparing for and then carrying out attacks is similar across terrorist groups. For example, a terrorist motivated by left-wing ideology explains how strategy – or politics as he referred to it – is translated into attacks:

*'The first decision is political – determining appropriate and possible targets. Once a set of targets is decided on, they must be reconnoitered and information gathered on how to approach the targets, how to place the bomb, how the security of the individuals and the explosives is to be protected. Then the time is chosen and a specific target. Next there was a preliminary run-through – in our case a number of practice sessions. Sometimes we don't do this as well as we should. The discipline during the actual operation is not to alter any of the agreed-upon plans or to discuss the action until everyone's safe within the group again. Our desire is not just for one success but to continue as long as possible.'*

Even though these last comments are more than 40 years old, they still apply just as much to terrorists active today as they did in 1970. Naturally, there is variation in settings, resources and weapons between groups and this produces variation in targets. Some groups are more experienced and skilled than others and enjoy better resources. Not surprisingly, their attacks tend to be more professional and sophisticated. Groups also tend to have preferred modus operandi – tactics and approaches in which they are experienced and which they use repeatedly even when other options are available.

The potential scale of terrorist attacks are limited at one level by the capability of the terrorist group, and there five key areas for considering a group's capability:

▶ **Quality of leadership** - leaders are crucial for effective organization, recruitment, group motivation, and refining and improving tactics and strategies. Leaders also play a critical role in highlighting appropriate targets and tactics for the movement as a whole.

▶ **Quantity of members** - the larger the number of members the group has, the more ambitious the group can be in terms of the number of operations it can mount (perhaps simultaneously), the complexity of these operations, and the level of intelligence and information the group can draw upon in planning and preparation. Greater numbers, though, also increase the risk of detection and infiltration by the security forces.

▶ **Quality of members** - the more experienced, better skilled, better trained and more highly motivated members are, the greater the capability the group possesses.

▶ **Weapons available** – this determines the types of target and tactics that are feasible.

▶ **Financial base** - the greater the funds available, the more sophisticated the types of operation a terrorist group can undertake. A lack of funds can force a group to divert increasing effort into fund-raising activities (which has its own risks and distractions).

As a result of real limits in capabilities – and with finite resources in time, money, information, skills and expertise – terrorist planning and preparation will never be perfect. Indeed, even dramatically successful terrorist attacks can still display failure and misjudgement by the perpetrators in the planning and execution stages (e.g. the failure of Flight 93 to reach its target on 9/11).

The second limit which applies just as strikingly to what terrorists do is more psychological. Ultimately, terrorist groups are conscious that there are boundaries to what they can do. These limits are effectively imposed by their supporters and sympathisers. Certain tactics can be used and certain targets selected only provided that the support base for the movement tolerates them. Consider, for example, this very telling comment from Eamon Collins, who for several years was an intelligence officer in the Provisional IRA:

> 'The IRA – regardless of their public utterances dismissing the condemnations of their behaviour from church and community leaders – tried to act in a way that would avoid severe censure from within the nationalist community; they knew they were operating within a sophisticated set of informal restrictions on their behaviour, no less powerful for being largely unspoken.'

The implication is that the terrorists must behave in an acceptable manner or else they will be rejected by their supporters (and potential supporters) and thus ruined. Comments such as Collins' clearly indicate that this is a fact very much to the forefront of terrorist thinking. Even Al-Qaeda, an organization which has shown itself to be repeatedly willing to kill very large numbers of civilians, operates within such a set of restrictions. Consider the following extracts from a letter written by Ayman al-Zawahiri to another terrorist commander criticizing the excessive violence of some of that commander's attacks and actions:

> 'the mujahed movement must avoid any action that the masses do not understand or approve ... the general opinion of our supporter does not comprehend that ... And we should spare the people from the effect of questions about the usefulness of our actions in the hearts and minds of the general opinion that is essentially sympathetic to us. ... I say to you: that we are in a battle, and that more than half of this battle is taking place in the battlefield of the media. And that we are in a media battle in a race for the hearts and minds of our Umma ... [we must not expose] ourselves to the questions and answering to doubts [among the Umma]. We don't need this.'

Zawahiri himself ordered some extremely ruthless acts in his time, but here he was trying to drive home the damaging impact of the other commander's extreme attacks in terms of undermining wider support for the movement.

Terrorism, fundamentally, is about influence. It revolves around the attempt of a small group of people to profoundly influence the lives of considerably larger groups. Violence and the threat of violence is the method through which this attempt is made, but in order to have its desired impact, people need to be aware of what is happening. Without awareness, there can be no impact.

Almost every terrorist group of the past century has been intensely concerned with the impact it has on the media. Most of them recognize that there is a vital media dimension to the conflict and terrorists usually recognize this more quickly and more intensely than their government opponents.

▲ An iconic image of a Black September terrorist during the 1972 Munich Olympics hostage crisis.

For terrorists, an attack which receives a great deal of media attention is usually seen as much more successful than an attack which receives relatively little (even if the human casualties and physical damage caused by both attacks are similar). Indeed, even if an attack results in the death or capture of all the terrorists involved, it can be still be regarded as highly successful if it has received intense media attention. Consider the following assessment from Abu 'Ubeid al-Qurashi, an Al-Qaeda activist who was looking back to the impact of the Black September attack on the 1972 Munich Olympics:

'Seemingly, the [Munich Olympics] operation failed because it did not bring about the release of the prisoners, and even cast a shadow of doubt on the justness of the Palestinian cause in world public opinion. But following the operation, and contrary to how it appeared [at first], it was the greatest media victory, and the first true proclamation to the entire world of the birth of the Palestinian resistance movement … In truth, the Munich operation was a great propaganda strike. Four thousand journalists and radio personnel, and two thousand commentators and television technicians were there to cover the Olympic Games; suddenly, they were broadcasting the suffering of the Palestinian people. Thus, 900 million people in 100 countries were witness to the operation by means of television screens. This meant that at least a quarter of the world knew what was going on in Munich; after this, they could no longer ignore the Palestinian tragedy. … There are data attesting to the importance of the Munich operation in the history of the resistance movement, and the extent of its influence on the entire world. It is known that a direct consequence of this operation was that thousands of young Palestinians were roused to join the fedayeen organizations … The number of organizations engaging in international "terror" increased from a mere 11 in 1968 to 55 in 1978. Fifty-four per cent of these new organizations sought to imitate the success of the Palestinian organization – particularly the publicity the Palestinian cause garnered after Munich.'

# 4

# What causes terrorism?

*Most revolutions are not caused by revolutionaries in the first place, but by the stupidity and brutality of governments.*

Sean MacStiofain, Provisional IRA chief of staff

ALL THAT
MATTERS

Understanding how and why terrorism begins is a vital first step towards preventing new campaigns erupting in the future. There is also the case that understanding what caused the violence in the first place will help to identify effective solutions and provide sensible guidance on how to wind down on-going violence.

Traditionally, efforts to understand what causes terrorism have tended to group together two very different issues:

▶ what it is that leads to terrorist campaigns starting in the first place

▶ what causes individuals to *join* terrorist groups.

Indeed, most of the work that is supposed to be about the causes of terrorism has really only focused on why people join. While many view these questions as being essentially the same thing, in reality they are two very different issues.

To illustrate just how different these questions can be, consider, for example, that we wanted to understand what causes wars to start between countries. One approach is to focus on identifying the factors that lead to wars breaking out. If we followed the terrorism model, the second approach is to explore why people join the military. You could have an excellent understanding of why recruits join the military but this would not necessarily shed any serious light on why wars start in the first place. Indeed, research on why wars happen generally has identified that the key factors are ones which have nothing to do with why people enlist in the military.

In comparison, terrorism researchers have become lulled into thinking that the recruitment process – or 'radicalization' as it is increasingly referred to – is a critical element in understanding the causes of terrorism. This is a mistake. Understanding why one person has become a terrorist does not necessarily tell you why an entire movement has turned to violence or how a campaign of terrorism started in the first place.

These two issues – causes and recruitment – are pulled apart here. Chapter 5 will focus on recruitment, how people come to support and join terrorist groups, what radicalization is and how it works. That is the individual perspective and much of my own work interviewing current and former terrorists has focused on exactly these questions. First, however, this chapter looks at the bigger issue of what it is that initially sets off terrorist campaigns.

Ten years ago there were formidable challenges facing anyone who wanted a serious answer to that question. There was a profound lack of meaningful research to shed light on the matter; this lack of data helps explain why experts tended to get sucked so easily into questions around recruitment. Most accounts usually drew on a small number of conflicts. These conflicts – and especially those in Northern Ireland and between the Palestinians and Israelis – had a tremendous influence as so many researchers focused on them. The apparent causes of these conflicts gradually came to be seen as the general causes of terrorism.

While these case studies provided important insights, it is dangerous to assume too much based on a very small number of cases. The available evidence has improved enormously in recent years. New studies based on assessing large numbers of conflicts have challenged some of the deeply held beliefs about the causes of terrorism and have also focused attention on some previously ignored issues. It is likely that research in the coming years will continue to refine and deepen our understanding but for now we are already able to tackle some long-standing myths and come to meaningful conclusions on the forces that create and encourage terrorism. First, let us deal with some of the myths.

## ▶ Poverty is *not* a root cause of terrorism

Arguably no myth is more widely believed than that poverty is a major driving force behind most terrorist conflicts. That this myth took hold is understandable. Poverty *appears* to be an issue in so many conflicts. The two most influential cases – Northern Ireland and Palestine – both flag it up as an important factor. Roman Catholics in Northern Ireland were on average significantly poorer than their Protestant neighbours. To an even starker extent, Palestinians are massively poorer on average than Israelis. Similar splits can be found in other conflicts. It was not surprising, then, that most commentators identified poverty as a significant cause of terrorism. Tied in with this is the equally widely believed myth that if poverty can be tackled or reduced, it will have a direct benefit in terms of reducing terrorism.

Tackling poverty is a worthwhile cause in its own right, but recent research has cast serious doubt on the view that poverty is a direct cause of terrorism.

If poverty was a direct cause, then surely most terrorists could reasonably be expected to come from poor backgrounds, and terrorism itself should be more common in poorer regions? Neither of these is true. Terrorism occurs across a spread of countries ranging from the richest nations to the most deprived. The table below shows the ten countries which suffered the highest levels of casualties as a result of terrorism between 1986 and 2002. This list includes some of the world's richest countries, which boast very high levels of GDP per capita. None of the countries on the list could be described as desperately poor.

▼ Top ten countries suffering casualties due to terrorism 1986–2002

| Country | Casualties 1986–2002 | Average GDP per capita 1986–2002 | 2001 Human Development Index rank |
|---|---|---|---|
| | | US$ | |
| Kenya | 5,365 | 1,211 | 123 (Medium) |
| United States | 4,011 | 27,816 | 6 (High) |
| India | 2,779 | 2,358 | 115 (Medium) |
| Israel-Palestine | 2,257 | 12,651 | 49 (High) |
| Sri Lanka | 1,815 | 3,365 | 81 (Medium) |
| Iraq | 1,646 | 3,413 | 106 (Medium) |
| Russian Federation | 1,314 | 8,377 | 60 (Medium) |
| Saudi Arabia | 1,037 | 10,348 | 68 (Medium) |
| United Kingdom | 984 | 19,627 | 14 (High) |
| Colombia | 835 | 5,615 | 62 (Medium) |

*Source*: Piazza, 2006

Further, it is widely recognized that relatively few terrorists come from the most deprived backgrounds of their own communities. On the contrary, they are much more likely to come from what constitutes the middle and upper classes of their communities (bearing in mind that the middle class in a refugee camp will be very different from the middle class in a British city). Surveys have also found that support for terrorism tends to be stronger among the middle and upper classes than among the lower class. For example, a survey of 1,357 Palestinian adults in the West Bank and Gaza found that support for terrorism against Israeli civilians was stronger among professionals (43.3 per cent) than among labourers (34.6 per cent). Similarly, there was more support among those with secondary education (39.4 per cent) than among illiterate respondents (32.3 per cent). Interestingly, surveys elsewhere in the Middle East found that people who owned a computer or mobile phone were much more likely to express support for terrorism than respondents who did not own these items.

# ▶ But rapid economic growth *is*

Tying in with the widely held belief that poverty is a major root cause of terrorism, there is an equally common expectation that times of economic hardship – depression or recession – will be associated with a rise in extremism and terrorism. In reality, it is not hard times that are associated with a rise in terrorism but rather periods of rapid growth and modernization, when the economy in theory seems to be entering a golden age. Rapid growth in GDP has been found to be a good predictor of an increase in ideologically motivated extremism (although it does not seem to have much impact on ethno-nationalist terrorism).

This finding is echoed in research into the causes of full-scale wars, which reveals that conflict between states is much more likely to occur during periods of economic growth rather than during depressions when times are hard. The historian Geoffrey Blainey argues that this is because the boom times give governments more resources to play with, and the expense of a war seems more bearable. In contrast, during economic downturns 'the mood of governments tends to be cautious or apprehensive'.

# ▶ Big populations, big problems

The larger the population of a country the more likely it is to suffer from terrorism. Indeed, population size alone is by far the most accurate single predictor of terrorism we have. The effects of all other predictors are massively increased if they occur in a country with a big population.

Why does population size matter? Two issues are probably important. First, the bigger the population the harder it becomes for the State to keep track of everyone, including potential extremists. Sprawling cities with massive populations provide melting pots for extremists and radicals to disappear into. Second, there is a simple numbers game in operation. While the overall number of people in any population who are prepared to become terrorists is tiny, as the size of the population increases, so does the number of potential terrorists. Terrorist campaigns can be carried out by isolated loners or disconnected small groups, so the risk inevitably rises as the overall population increases.

If we look at the number of people convicted of terrorist activities in Western countries, we can get an indication of how this works. Between 2006 and 2010, the 25 countries of the European Union convicted a total of 1,673 people for terrorism-related activity. The convictions were not, however, evenly spread across the region. Thirteen countries had *no* convictions whatsoever, and another four had fewer than 20. At the other end of the spectrum, one country was responsible for almost half of all convictions – Spain, with a total of 744. The United Kingdom was next with 365.

Clearly it would be sloppy thinking to assume that every active terrorist was caught and convicted in this time period. Drawing on past conflicts, there is some evidence to suggest that for every two terrorists convicted, there will be *roughly* five people engaged in terrorist activity still outside the criminal justice system. This figure is likely to be very generous with regard to some terrorist groups, but for the sake of argument we will run with it. This would suggest that in total across the 25 European countries covered, with a combined population of over 468 million, there were no more than 4,200 people actively involved in some form of terrorist activity (including those who ended up convicted in court). This means that out of every 112,000 people living in these countries, just one was involved in terrorist activity at some point during the five years. For countries with the most serious problems the ratios were not quite as good. In Spain, for example, the ratio dropped to one in 24,813 people, while in the UK the figure was one in 68,385.

The central lesson, though, is clear. While terrorists are exceptionally rare in populations – in the UK, for example, they are considerably rarer than full-time professional footballers (who outnumber them ten to one) – as the overall population size increases, so does the pool of potential terrorists. The larger the population, the higher the number of potential terrorists.

Some have suggested that perhaps it is not a question of population size, but rather how crowded the population is. The extreme overcrowding in Gaza, for example, is highlighted as a case in point. Gaza certainly is badly overcrowded. It ranks sixth in the world for regional population density, with a current level of 4,750 people per square kilometre. Some critics counter with the argument that there are cities elsewhere with much higher population densities than this and that the plight of Gaza is overstated. These critics, though, generally overlook the fact that the cities they cite as examples do not have Gaza's severely restricted transport links with the wider world, and neither do they suffer from Gaza's crumbling infrastructure and profoundly limited access to surrounding countryside and waterways.

Both Singapore and Hong Kong, for example, are much more crowded than Gaza, but both of these cities have a first-rate infrastructure and excellent transport links. Their ability to cope with their massive populations is in a completely different league to that seen in Gaza. In raw economic terms Singapore, for example, is able to import over $304 billion worth of materials and goods each year. In contrast, Gaza struggles to bring in even $1.5 billion (and almost a third of this has to be smuggled in through an extensive tunnel system). Pound for pound the cost to import material into Gaza is three times higher than for Singapore. Cement, crucial for housing and infrastructure, costs $185 per tonne in Gaza (and at one stage in recent years cost well over $300 per tonne); in Singapore it costs just $63 per tonne. We could go further but the essential point is that overcrowding presents a far more massive problem for Gaza than it does for those few cities which have higher population densities. Even so, overcrowding by itself does not seem to produce terrorism. Looking across a wide range of different regions we find that while the raw population size is a good predictor of terrorism, population density is an extremely poor one.

# ▶ Civil liberties and human rights

The more repressive a state becomes, the more likely it is that terrorism will emerge. Repression can be measured in a number of ways but can include the loss of civil liberties, the restriction of freedom of expression and an increase in human rights abuses. In a study looking at the experience of 97 countries over a 20-year period, it was found that those countries which became increasingly repressive during this time were also the ones most likely to witness the outbreak of terrorist violence. Overall, the level of human rights abuses in a country is a far stronger predictor of terrorism than any of the economic-related measures that have been proposed.

# ▶ Lack of political representation

Countries which curtail or severely restrict democratic politics are much more likely to produce internal terrorism. A simple measure of how many political parties are represented in the law-making institutions of government provides a surprisingly good predictor of future terrorism. The lower the number of parties which are present, the more likely it is that domestic terrorism will occur. Similarly, a lack of representation in other arenas (such as a lack of workers' trade unions) also shows a link with increased violent extremism. In short, the more curtailed political representation is in any given society the greater the risk of domestic terrorism erupting in that culture.

# ▶ The failure of existing political movements

Many terrorist groups have their direct origins in more mainstream political movements which have failed or stagnated. The Russian group Narodnaya Volya discussed in Chapter 2 emerged from the ashes of a much larger student movement. Most of these political movements are advocating change through conventional politics or non-violent methods. If these tactics appear to be failing, however, this can lead to a crisis within the movement which either produces a significant change in strategy (frequently accompanied by a change of leadership) or a split in the movement with a more hard-line element breaking away from the main organization.

Splits within existing political movements can be a warning sign of trouble ahead. Whenever splits occur there will inevitably be less extreme and more extreme factions. The less extreme faction will typically advocate continuing to adopt the established non-violent methods to bring about change. The more extreme faction, however, may be so disillusioned with such approaches that they now embrace aggressive policies. The result can be a rapid adoption of terrorism in the aftermath of a split. In many cases the origins of a terrorist campaign can be traced to a split in what was previously a larger – but essentially peaceful – movement. Terrorist groups with such origins include the Tamil Tigers in Sri Lanka, the INLA in Northern Ireland, and FARC and M-19 in Columbia.

In some cases it is possible for the legitimate group to move towards terrorism even without a clear split occurring. For example, Shining Path in Peru and GRAPO in Spain are both examples of mainstream movements which drifted towards terrorism following the failure of the group to achieve its aims through non-violent methods. In these cases, such a change of direction was often preceded by a change in the organization's senior leadership, with more aggressive leaders emerging to take over from more moderate figures.

# ▶ Catalyst events

Perceived injustices are important drivers of individual decisions to become involved in militant activism. Catalyst events (i.e. violent acts which are perceived to be unjust) provide a strong sense of outrage and a powerful psychological desire for revenge and retribution. Sometimes these are also referred to as 'trigger events'.

Normally a catalyst event is an act of extreme physical violence committed by the police or security forces or other rival group against the individual, or their family, friends or anyone they identify strongly with. The shooting of a father and his 12-year-old son by Israeli soldiers in September 2000 at Netzarim acted as such a catalyst event for Palestinians. Captured on television, the shooting of the two as they cowered behind a water barrel contributed to a dramatic resurgence in terrorist violence in the region.

▲ Bloody Sunday, Northern Ireland, 1972. The shooting of unarmed Catholics by the British army led to a flood of recruits for the IRA.

In Northern Ireland, Bloody Sunday stands out as an example of such a catalyst. In January 1972, 13 Catholics were shot dead by the British Army while taking part in a civil rights march in Derry. A 14th victim died later of his injuries. Seven of the dead were teenagers. Initially the government tried to create the impression that the soldiers had come under fire first and that some of the dead may have been carrying weapons. These allegations ultimately proved groundless. After Bloody Sunday, IRA violence escalated alarmingly in the region. In the three years before that day, some 250 people had been killed in the conflict. In the 12 months which followed, nearly 500 people died.

# ▶ Contagion and media effects

The outbreak of terrorism in one country increases the risk that terrorist conflicts will also erupt in neighbouring countries. The terrorist groups are not necessarily the same; rather it seems that the example of the neighbour inspires radical groups in nearby countries to also take violent action. The media plays an important role in this contagion process. Perhaps the best recent example of contagion in action can be seen with the Arab Spring which began in December 2010. Massive public protests broke out first in Tunisia, then Egypt and then rapidly spread to several other countries in North Africa and the Middle East. In Tunisia, within a month the protests led to the collapse of the ruling government. In other cases, such as Egypt, the unrest endured for much longer and involved a much higher level of violence as autocratic regimes fought to hold on to power. In every case the existing regimes repeatedly referred to the protestors as 'terrorists'. In Egypt the regime eventually collapsed. Elsewhere the unrest led to full-blown civil wars, some of which are still continuing. Only in countries with small populations have the old regimes so far seemed capable of crushing the initial waves of dissent. Social media played a critical role in the inspiration and organization of the different protest movements. The successive government collapses in Tunisia, Egypt and Libya worked to fuel unrest in nearby regions. In a similar fashion – though usually not quite so dramatic – contagion can spread smaller scale terrorist campaigns across neighbouring regions.

The ability of the media to spread terrorism has not always been accepted by experts. Initial research on the subject failed to find a clear link between media coverage and a rise in terrorism. While it was often assumed that media coverage did lead to more terrorism, the evidence for this in the 1970s and 1980s was very weak. What was found, however, was a clear contagion effect: terrorism tactics which received more coverage were more likely to be copied in the future. The overall number of attacks was unchanged, but terrorist groups did show a shift towards the types of attacks which received more media attention.

More recent research has suggested the effect is now even stronger, possibly due to the impact of 24-hour news channels, the internet and social media. A review of terrorist attacks from 1998 to 2004 suggested that increased coverage was followed by an increase in the overall amount of terrorism. Further, the link seems to be reciprocal: more attacks leads to more coverage, and more coverage was then followed by a further increase in attacks.

Overall, the evidence available today suggests that two effects exist:

▶ a contagion effect – increased media coverage of a particular type of terrorist tactic leads to an increase in similar types of attacks being carried out

▶ a magnitude effect – more coverage is linked to more attacks happening overall.

Exactly how strong these effects are is still not entirely clear, especially given the mixed nature of some findings. Nevertheless, given the intense interest the media often shows in terrorism, the findings make for sobering thought.

# ▶ Summary

The past ten years have transformed our understanding of what the causes of terrorism really are, and it is very likely that the next ten years will continue to refine our insights. Research has in some cases confirmed long-held ideas, but a number of widely assumed 'causes' have been discredited, while a few previously unsuspected factors have been revealed. The result is a genuine transformation in what we know about the origins of terrorism. The consistent lesson, however, is that one factor by itself is rarely enough. Instead, as the range of factors increases in a region, then it becomes more inevitable that a terrorist conflict will erupt.

Having considered the causes behind terrorism in general, Chapter 5 looks at why people are willing to join terrorist groups and engage in campaigns of often extreme and brutal violence.

# 5

# Inside the terrorist mind

*Hatred is an element of the struggle; a relentless hatred of the enemy, impelling us over and beyond the natural limitations that man is heir to and transforming him into an effective, violent, selective and cold killing machine. Our soldiers must be thus; a people without hatred cannot vanquish a brutal enemy.*

*Ernesto 'Che' Guevara*

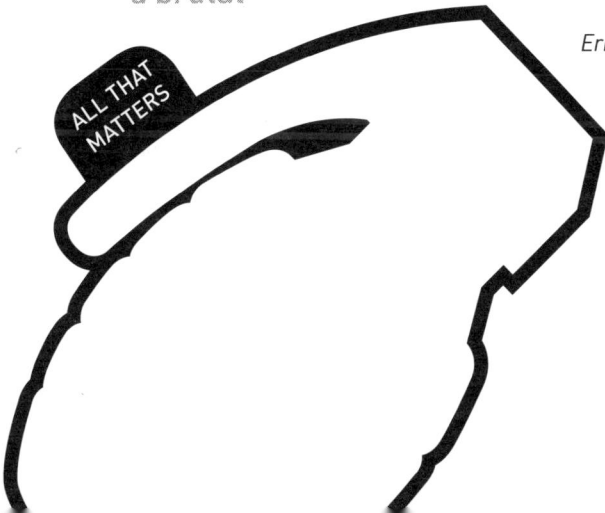

ALL THAT
MATTERS

As a psychologist, the question I am asked most about terrorists is 'why do they do it?' This question – more than any other – troubles not only members of the public, but also scientists and policy-makers. The obsession with finding the answer has come to dominate the whole debate over the causes of terrorism.

In the post-9/11 world, understanding how people become terrorists has come to be discussed in terms of 'radicalization', an exotic term which presumably describes a similarly exotic process. What is called radicalization today, in the past was referred to much more mundanely as 'joining' a terrorist group or being 'recruited'. No one talked of the IRA being 'radicalized', or Shining Path, or ETA or the Red Army Faction. Though they all certainly were according to our modern understanding. After 9/11 it became awkward to talk about people 'becoming' terrorists, 'joining' terrorist groups or being 'recruited'. Those terms were too banal, too ordinary. Ordinary terms might imply ordinary processes, and worse, ordinary solutions. They had to make way for something more exotic, more extreme. 'Radicalization' fitted the bill nicely. Only slowly has there been a growing realization that this new term might hinder our ability to understand terrorists at least as much as it helps.

# ▶ Are terrorists crazy?

Terrorist violence can be extreme. Some attacks show profound levels of ruthlessness and barbarity. In considering such deeds it is natural to wonder at the psychology of the perpetrators and ask what mechanisms allow people to do this to their fellows. One easy answer is to assume that the perpetrators are insane and that their psychology is profoundly different from the rest of us. Terrorists, then, belong in a similar camp to sadistic serial killers and mass murderers: the products of disturbed childhoods, faulty genes and serious personality disorders. In short, they are not normal; they are crazy, dangerous people and this is why they are engaged in terrorism.

This is an old argument, one which has been offered up to explain virtually every terrorist movement in history. Recall Josephus 2,000 years ago describing the motivation of the Sicarii as 'the madness of desperate men'. It appeals to our instinctive beliefs that extreme acts require extreme actors. Ordinary people do not do extraordinary things. There *must* be something different about the terrorist.

It comes as a shock, then, to hear that the vast majority of psychological research on terrorists has concluded that they are not abnormal and that there is no distinct terrorist personality. Not only are they not different, but many studies have found that terrorists are actually psychologically much healthier and far more stable than other violent criminals. An act of extreme violence does not in itself show that the perpetrator is psychologically distinct from the rest of humanity. While a few psychologists continue to believe terrorists are mentally abnormal, their conclusions are based on very weak evidence (and for the most part these psychologists have never actually met a terrorist). Psychologists and psychiatrists who have met and assessed terrorists face-to-face have nearly always concluded that these people were in no way abnormal and instead have surprisingly stable and rational personalities. The consensus is that, where it occurs, such abnormality is the exception rather than the rule, and is more likely to be found in people on the fringe of terrorist movements.

Overall, terrorists are a very heterogeneous group and the range of people – both men and women – who become involved is vast. They can vary hugely in terms of education, family background, age, intelligence, economic class, etc. Consequently the manner in which they became a terrorist can also vary, and factors that played a pivotal role in one person's decision to engage in terrorism may play only a very minor role for others, or indeed no part at all.

▲ Timothy McVeigh (centre), responsible for the Oklahoma City bombing in 1995 which killed 168 people. How can ordinary people engage in extreme violence?

Despite this diversity, four decades of research have shown that a number of factors appear to be relatively common in the backgrounds of terrorists. Becoming a terrorist is, for most people, a gradual process and not usually something that happens quickly or easily. Ultimately, it is the combined impact of a number of factors that push and pull the individual into violent extremism, and these factors will vary depending on the culture, the social context, the terrorist group and the person involved.

# ▶ Understanding radicalization

While radicalization is a flawed concept – and in troubling ways means different things to different people – we are stuck with it as a term for the moment (much as we are stuck with 'terrorism'). Research on the radicalization process indicates that it normally takes between four months and two years for an individual to become radicalized to the point where they are willing to carry out a terrorist attack. A number of psychological factors have been identified as potentially important in this process.

To begin with, becoming a terrorist is in the first instance an issue of socialization. Frequently terrorists do not join as isolated individuals. Rather, it is within small groups that individuals gradually become radicalized. In his analysis of the life histories of hundreds of jihadi terrorists, Edwin Bakker found that these individuals tended to become involved through networks of friends or relatives. In short, the individuals were not becoming radicalized because of the efforts of an Al-Qaeda recruiter but, surprisingly, the process was effectively occurring independent of the terrorist organization.

The potential recruits gradually adopt the beliefs and faith of their more extreme friends and associates. Over time, they become more distant from childhood friends and family who are not involved, and grow increasingly dependent on and loyal to the extremist group. With the increasing focus on this group, the ideals and values of the movement become even more important and intense. Combined with an increased sense of group identity and commitment, this helps to radicalize individuals and facilitate their entry into violent extremism in a way that is encouraged and sanctioned by their new social peers.

Any given society possesses some minorities and other disaffected groups who, rightly or wrongly, perceive the world as treating them harshly. In some cases, there are genuine and very substantial causes for grievance. Individuals who belong to or identify with such disaffected groups share in a sense of injustice and persecution. It is from such pools that individual terrorists emerge. The move from the disaffected to violent extremist is often facilitated by the type of catalyst events discussed in Chapter 4.

Crucially, one does not need to experience such events first-hand to be affected by them. Vicarious exposure through television or the internet can have an almost equally strong impact. In the past, IRA members who came from the Irish Republic often reported that it was what they had seen on television which motivated them to join the group. They had no relatives or friends living in Northern Ireland – and most had never even been there or seen a British soldier or policeman in real life – but media coverage of the violence had played a critical role in convincing them to join. Similarly, today, most militant jihadi recruits have never been to regions such as Iraq, Afghanistan or Israel. They have no direct connections with those countries, no friends or family living there. However, they do have a sense of connection with the conflict, and the media coverage of the conflict – combined with the often graphic coverage in jihadi propaganda videos – acts as an important catalyst in the radicalization process.

In terms of trying to develop a deeper understanding of the psychology of extremism – and support for extremism – some additional psychological factors have been identified as potentially important and useful. We will consider some of these now.

## Aggression

Aggressiveness as a trait has certainly been linked to criminal violence. Overall, it is a relatively stable trait which is largely consistent across time and situations, and is a very good predictor of criminal violence. For example, children who are rated as aggressive at the ages of eight and ten are three times more likely to be convicted of a violent crime as an adult.

There has been some speculation as to whether aggression may also be a factor in determining who is more likely to join terrorist groups and support such violence. A survey of nearly 7,000 Palestinian schoolchildren in Gaza and the West Bank asked the children if they had been involved in the first intifada. The survey found a significant correlation between those who admitted being involved and measures of aggression.

At face value, this result can be taken as evidence that more aggressive individuals are indeed more likely to engage in political violence. However, some caution is needed as involvement in the intifada was measured by just one question, which asked:

> 'Before the withdrawal of Israeli troops from the Gaza Strip and Jericho, did you ever distribute leaflets, protect someone from Israeli soldiers or police, march or demonstrate against the occupation, and throw stones at Israeli soldiers?'

The answer to this question was 'yes' or 'no'. As can be seen, the question covered a very wide range of behaviours and did not differentiate between violent activity and non-violent activity. Nevertheless, aggression remains a potentially important factor which is worth further attention in future research.

# Altruism

Perhaps strangely, many terrorists may see their involvement in terrorism as a pro-social activity rather than an anti-social activity (as it is often deemed by others).

Some anecdotal evidence supports this view and suggests that terrorists may score higher on measures of altruism than others. Altruism is a desire to help or assist others, and a key element in understanding altruism is empathy. Empathy allows individuals to appreciate the world from someone else's point of view. The more strongly an individual identifies with another person or group of people, the more strongly they will react emotionally to events in the life of that person or group. They will feel positive emotions when things go well for that person, and negative emotions when things go badly. These negative emotions include sadness but also, importantly, can include anger.

Altruistic tendencies can be increased by stressing similarities with others. The more strongly a person can identify with others, the more they care about what happens to them. In contrast, stressing the differences weakens such bonds, and interest and concern declines. A further important factor in limiting altruistic tendencies is that if an individual is burdened with extreme demands on their own time, energy and resources, they are much less likely to be able to show the awareness that altruism requires.

Thus the capacity to exercise altruistic tendencies links in with many of the theories regarding poverty and deprivation and terrorism which we discussed earlier. It is widely recognized that most terrorists do not come from the most deprived backgrounds; on the contrary, they are more likely to come from what constitutes the middle and upper classes of their own communities.

Altruism is likely to have an impact on support for terrorism when it is considered within the context of identity. Individuals who feel their identity is closer to the militant group, and who score higher on altruistic measures, are arguably the ones who will express and feel the strongest support for the group, including the group's use of extreme measures. Potentially, they will also be more likely to act on these sentiments.

# Deindividuation

Deindividuation is a psychological state in which inner restraints are lost when people are not seen or paid attention to as individuals. This loss of restraint can lead to behaviour becoming less altruistic, more selfish and more aggressive. Individuals can become more impulsive and less concerned with what others might think about their behaviour. Not surprisingly, deindividuation has been linked with a range of criminal and deviant activity, including stealing, cheating, violence and murder. It is also believed to play a role in the psychology of terrorist cells.

Deindividuation can be caused by a number of factors, with perceived anonymity being one of the key causes. A great deal of research has demonstrated that individuals who believe their identity is unknown are more likely to behave in an aggressive and punitive manner. The conditions found in many terrorist groups – in particular their intensely clandestine nature, but also aspects such as the strong group identity, strong pressure to conform, high levels of risk and stress – are all likely to produce deindividuation. As a result, an individual's normal inhibitions about engaging in serious violence  can be seriously weakened and eroded, even when women and children will be the victims.

# Mortality salience

When people are exposed to death-related thoughts or imagery, this results in what psychologists refer to as a 'mortality salience' effect. Research has found that even very subtle cues relating to death – cues that are not consciously recognized by the person involved – can create a mortality salience effect.

Mortality salience results in people feeling an increasing pride in and identification with their country, religion, gender, race, etc. They experience exaggerated tendencies to stereotype and reject those who are different from themselves. The group you belong to is even better than it was before, even more worthy of your support. Your rivals are diminished, less deserving of sympathy or compassion. Hostility toward those who are perceived as different increases.

These changes in attitude and perceptions are also linked to changes in behaviour. Some of these are relatively subtle, such as sitting closer to a person who shares your own culture, while moving further away from foreigners. Others are starker, including increased physical aggression toward anyone critical of important beliefs.

Crucially, mortality salience has also been found to lead to an increase in support for extremism when it is linked to group identity. One study found that under mortality salience conditions, white Americans expressed more sympathy and support for other whites who expressed racist views. In the Middle East, Muslim students under mortality salience conditions expressed more support and sympathy for suicide bombers, and also expressed a greater willingness to carry out suicide attacks themselves.

The more that important cultural icons and beliefs are involved – in the context of militant jihadi terrorism, examples might be reference to the Qur'an, the Prophet Mohammed and other vital aspects of Islam – the more pronounced the effect is likely to be. As already indicated, mortality salience leads to an increased attachment and protectiveness towards such beliefs, and also produces increased hostility and aggression towards those who appear to be denigrating or insulting such icons and beliefs. Stories such as the alleged abuse of copies of the Qur'an committed by Americans in Iraq and Afghanistan, for example, take on a more serious and provocative dimension under mortality salience conditions.

# ◗ Concluding thoughts

The key to terrorist psychology seems to depend far more on understanding ordinary psychological processes than on assuming that terrorists are unique or crazy. The realization that terrorist psychology is not significantly different from anyone else's is a cause for both hope and despair. It gives hope because it highlights the crucial role that environment plays in determining whether people become terrorists or not, and it gives us some targets to aim at when trying to prevent radicalization. The despair comes with the realization that in the wrong circumstances most people could either come to support a terrorist group or even consider joining one. Fortunately, most of us will never live in such circumstances and will not face such choices.

# 6

# Suicide terrorism

*Who scorns his own life is
lord of yours.*

*Seneca*

In the 20th century, suicide terrorism was a peripheral tactic, exotic, carried out sporadically by a handful of groups. Barely one terrorist attack in every 100,000 used suicide tactics, and the phenomenon was considered more of a curiosity than a serious strategic problem. With the passing of the old millennium, all of that changed. As the graph below illustrates, there has been a staggering increase in suicide terrorism since 2000. Suicide attacks now account for around 5 per cent of all incidents; more importantly, almost one third of all the people killed by terrorists in the years since 2000 have died as a result of suicide attacks (over 25,000 dead and the number is still rising). On average, each suicide attack will have 40 casualties; non-suicide attacks average less than five. More than any other terrorist tactic, suicide assaults are the ones most likely to kill the terrorists' intended targets and are also the strikes most difficult to defend against. Quite simply, suicide attacks are the most potent tactic in the modern terrorist's arsenal and the number of terrorist groups willing to use these methods has grown rapidly in recent years.

Yet, suicide terrorism is not a new phenomenon. It has a history which can be traced back for thousands of years. Accounts of individuals sacrificing their lives in order to kill their enemies are found in the Old Testament. In the 11th century an Islamic sect, the Ismal'ili Shi'ites (better known to history as the Assassins), launched a 200-year-long campaign of terrorism using suicide attackers. The modern age of suicide terrorism effectively began in 1983, when terrorists launched a series of suicide strikes against foreign targets in Lebanon. They first destroyed the US embassy and then launched a devastating attack on the US Marine barracks in Beirut. Also destroyed was a building housing French paratroopers. Over 300 people were killed in these assaults. In the aftermath, Western countries hastily pulled all their forces out of the country and effectively abandoned the region for years. For terrorists across the world, the attacks may have been extreme but they also represented a simple and cheap tactic capable of getting even the most powerful military forces in the world to back off.

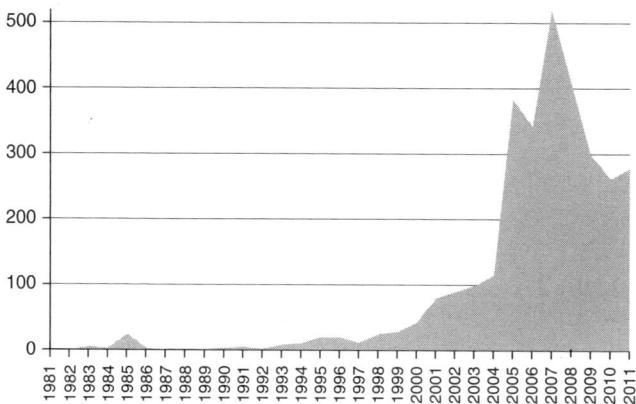

▲ The rise of suicide terrorism 1981–2011

Not surprisingly, other groups began to copy what had happened. Some of these groups, like Hamas and Islamic Jihad, shared the same religious orientation. But many non-Muslim groups also adopted the tactics: Christian terrorists started using suicide assaults against the Israeli army in south Lebanon; Hindu Tamils became especially adept with such methods in Sri Lanka and India, and the Marxist PKK in Turkey tried their hand at suicide attacks when things became especially desperate for them in the mid-1990s.

In Western minds, dominated by the images of planes slamming into the twin towers of the World Trade Center in 2001, suicide bombers seem easy to categorize. Young males, with fundamentalist Islamist views, who come primarily from Arab countries, are for most a reliable stereotype of the typical suicide bomber. Even so, the stereotype is a clumsy one. With so many different groups involved, each with their different conflicts, cultures, religions, ethnic backgrounds and agendas, the idea that there can be a single profile which fits the bombers of all groups quickly falls apart.

Even trying to pin suicide terrorism firmly to Islam dissolves with an examination of history. While there is a malaise in that great religion which has helped spur the rise of Al-Qaeda and its brethren, one does not need to draw upon the Qur'an alone to justify suicide attacks. Indeed, the first recorded instance of a suicide attack is not in an Islamic but a Jewish context. In the Bible, the Old Testament book of Judges provides a detailed account of the death of Samson, a Jewish 'judge' (leader) and hero. Captured by his enemies, the Philistines, the humiliated Samson was tortured, mutilated and blinded. Then the Old Testament describes how the Philistines brought Samson to their main hall so that he could be tortured further in public:

> 'And Samson said unto the lad that held him by the hand, Suffer me that I may feel the pillars whereupon the house standeth, that I may lean upon them. Now the house was full of men and women; and all the lords of the Philistines were there; and there were

*upon the roof about three thousand men and women, that beheld while Samson made sport. And Samson called unto the Lord, and said, O Lord God, remember me, I pray thee, and strengthen me, I pray thee, only this once, O God, that I may be at once avenged of the Philistines for my two eyes. And Samson took hold of the two middle pillars upon which the house stood, and on which it was borne up, of the one with his right hand, and of the other with his left. And Samson said, Let me die with the Philistines. And he bowed himself with all his might; and the house fell upon the lords, and upon all the people that were therein. So the dead which he slew at his death were more than they which he slew in his life.'*

▲ Samson collapses the main hall of the Philistines, killing himself and 3,000 of his enemies.

Thus, according to the Bible, in this one act of destruction Samson killed as many people (men, women and children, if the phrase 'lad' is an indication) as the 9/11 hijackers killed in their efforts in 2001. What is telling, however, is that the Bible does not condemn Samson's actions. On the contrary, Samson's suicide is presented as an act of redemption as well as of vengeance, which is interesting given the general Judaeo-Christian proscriptions of suicide. While the Bible in other places does prohibit killing and suicide, it is clear in this particular passage that Samson's actions were condoned. He asked God for strength and this was granted. Thus, for a Christian or Jew who questions whether suicide killing can be sanctioned by their religion, the story of Samson provides explicit evidence that it can (even when women and children are among the victims). Clearly, it is not just Islam which can provide mixed messages on this issue.

Close examination of almost all major cultures will throw up examples like Samson. Heroes who sacrifice themselves for a cause are a recurring motif in most human societies. Individuals and groups who resist in the face of hopeless odds and certain death are heralded as icons of courage and honour. Wider pride is taken from their defiance. Consider for example, the 300 Spartans who refused to surrender to a Persian army of perhaps 250,000 at the battle of Thermopylae in 480 BC. Even 2,500 years later, modern society continues to produce books and films about this battle, and in every case it is the Spartans who are portrayed as the heroes.

Suicide terrorists are in many respects the modern inheritors of this legacy. They and their supporters certainly see their actions as heroic, courageous and noble. One of the obstacles to understanding suicide killing is that if you do not sympathize with the cause, it is difficult to see the perpetrator as anything other than an evil psychopath, or at best as a vulnerable person who has been cynically manipulated and brainwashed. Yet if there is some sympathy with the cause, then such explanations begin to ring hollow.

For example, if through a suicide attack you could kill Adolf Hitler during the Second World War – and thus potentially end not only the war but also the genocide of the Holocaust – would you do it? What would you think of someone who did agree to do this? Would you think such a suicide bomber was a hero, sacrificing himself for what were clearly just and sufficient reasons? Or would you see him as a brainwashed fanatic, coerced or 'radicalized' into killing himself this way?

On 20 March 1943, a German army officer, Rudolph-Christoph von Gersdoff, faced just this dilemma. He was scheduled to escort Adolf Hitler and other leading Nazis through a museum exhibition in Berlin. Only a few days before the exhibition tour, Gersdoff was approached and asked if he would be willing to carry out a suicide attack in order to kill Hitler and the other Nazi leaders. He agreed to make the attempt.

On the day of the tour, Hitler arrived in the company of Göring, Himmler, Dönitz and Keitel. When Gersdoff saw Hitler approaching, he ignited the fuse to a bomb hidden under his clothes, and then kept close to the Führer as he walked among the exhibits. However, the rushed nature of the operation – involving as it did only a few days planning and preparation – had not given the plotters enough time to acquire a short fuse to detonate the explosives. Instead, Gersdoff had to use a ten-minute fuse. Gersdoff attempted to delay the Führer's progress by explaining the significance of the different exhibits, but Hitler showed little interest. He rushed through the halls. To everyone's surprise, after only two minutes the Führer left the building through a side door. Unable to follow, an appalled Gersdoff rushed to the nearest toilets, where he ripped out the fuse to the bomb.

So what do we make of Gersdoff? Was he misguided? Evil? A hero? Your immediate reaction will probably depend a great deal on how you view his cause. If you think that killing Hitler and the other senior Nazis was justified, Gersdoff's actions will seem more reasonable and acceptable, and his willingness to sacrifice himself in the attempt an indication of personal courage rather than madness.

Suicide terrorists today certainly believe that they are fighting an evil as great as the one Gersdoff saw in Hitler. As a result, they see suicide actions as both necessary and justified, and crucially they never describe the act as 'suicide'. Rather the language used is always in terms of *sacrificing* oneself for a serious and honourable cause. Psychologically this is an important distinction. Consider for example the following comments of Sheikh Yousef Al-Qaradhawi, a prominent Egyptian theologian:

> 'Those who oppose martyrdom operations and claim that they are suicide are making a great mistake. The goals of the one who carries out a martyrdom operation and of the one who commits suicide are completely different ... The suicide kills himself for himself, because he failed in business, love, an examination, or the like. He was too weak to cope with the situation and chose to flee life for death. In contrast, the one who carries out a martyrdom operation does not think of himself. He sacrifices himself for the sake of a higher goal, for which all sacrifices become meaningless.'

In most cases, the decision to carry out a suicide attack is not made quickly or abruptly. Rather, the journey is best seen as a gradual process. In most jihadi plots in the West, at least one member of the team has travelled overseas for training in the six-month period prior to the attack. It is not usual for all members to attend such overseas training together but normally the leader of the cell is among those who travel. This trip normally involves attending a training camp where skills appropriate to conducting an attack are taught and other preparations are made. The average time between returning from overseas training and the launching of an attack is just four months.

The choice to carry out a suicide attack is in most cases the most profound decision that bombers make in their lives. It is certainly the one with the most blatantly serious consequences. As a result, and not surprisingly, many bombers report being worried about this choice in the run-up to the attack. Many seek reassurance that the decision is the right one. A number of rituals help provide a framework to endorse suicide attacks, and to emphasize the special nature of what is to happen and, as a consequence, the special nature of the individual who is to carry out the act. Rituals can provide important psychological milestones to bolster commitment and also act as psychological points of no return. Perhaps the clearest indicator of this comes with the video recording of a last testament. For Palestinian suicide attackers this is usually filmed the day before an attack, but for Al-Qaeda it is more normal for it to be recorded a few months or weeks beforehand.

These messages are not intended primarily for family and friends but are aimed at a much wider and more public audience. This includes both supporters and sympathisers with the terrorists' cause but also opponents and those who may be relatively neutral about the struggle. The bombers and the organizations are aware that the videos will receive enormous media attention both nationally and internationally when they are released. Indeed, the video testimonies represent one of the most potent ways that terrorist groups can access the media.

In the 1990s and early 2000s, most video testimonies from groups such as Hamas and Hezbollah primarily involved the bomber simply reciting parts of the Qur'an. The video was constrained and very formalized. This began to change, however, in the 2000s as different groups sought to achieve a growing range of aims through the video footage. Increasingly bombers have focused on:

- highlighting that they know they are embarking on a suicide mission – ruling out the possibility that they were tricked or duped

- emphasizing that they volunteered or actively sought out the mission – trying to undermine the idea that they were coerced or pressured

- trying to highlight their own intelligence, education and skills in order to undermine the view that they were somehow brainwashed into carrying out the attack.

A good example of this type of footage comes from the video of Mohammad Sidique Khan, the leader of the suicide bombers responsible for the 7 July 2005 attacks in London:

> *'I'm going to keep this short and to the point because it's all been said before by far more eloquent people than me. And our words have no impact upon you, therefore I'm going to talk to you in a language that you understand. Our words are dead until we give them life with our blood.*
>
> *'I'm sure by now the media's painted a suitable picture of me, this predictable propaganda machine will naturally try to put a spin on things to suit the government and to scare the masses into conforming to their power and wealth-obsessed agendas.*
>
> *'I and thousands like me are forsaking everything for what we believe. Our driving motivation doesn't come from tangible commodities that this world has*

*to offer. Our religion is Islam – obedience to the one true God, Allah, and following the footsteps of the final prophet and messenger Muhammad ... This is how our ethical stances are dictated.*

*'Your democratically elected governments continuously perpetuate atrocities against my people all over the world. And your support of them makes you directly responsible, just as I am directly responsible for protecting and avenging my Muslim brothers and sisters.*

*'Until we feel security, you will be our targets. And until you stop the bombing, gassing, imprisonment and torture of my people we will not stop this fight. We are at war and I am a soldier. Now you too will taste the reality of this situation.'*

For the bomber, as well as fulfilling a significant propaganda role, the video testimony also becomes a major psychological milestone. Having filmed the video it becomes much more difficult for the bomber to back out of the operation. In some movements, once the film has been made, other group members refer to the bomber as *al-shahid al-hai*, 'the living martyr'. This means that the individual is already dead and is only temporarily in this world. After this stage, few pull out of the operation.

While interest varies, suicide attacks will always hold some attraction for terrorists. The ability of the tactic to circumvent so many traditional defence and security measures means that it will inevitably hold a special appeal for groups who are struggling to harm what they perceive to be well-defended and well-prepared opponents. This will be particularly the case where the root causes of the conflict are being exacerbated, where the loss of life is already high and where the terrorist group feels its own position is growing increasingly desperate. Ultimately, suicide terrorism can occur anywhere. If history is any guide, we are not likely ever to be entirely free from its threat and no country or region is entirely immune to the risk.

# 7

# Super terrorism

*Now I am become Death,
the destroyer of worlds.*

J. Robert Oppenheimer, *quoting the*
Bhagavad Gita *after the first atomic bomb test*

In January 2009, reports emerged from Algeria that at least 40 members of Al-Qaeda in the Land of Islamic Mahgreb (AQLIM) had been killed in the east of the country. The militants had not, however, died fighting with government forces but had been killed when an experiment to develop biological weapons went badly wrong. AQLIM were trying to develop a weaponized form of the bubonic plague, but lost control of the effort and infection spread rapidly among the group. The bodies and equipment were sealed in a cave and the militants' base was abandoned.

The incident was a sobering reminder of the interest terrorists have in weapons of mass destruction (WMD). Such weapons take four forms: chemical, biological, radiological and nuclear (CBRN). A recurring nightmare for governments around the world is that terrorists will try to use such weapons with a potential to kill on a scale that would dwarf the death toll of 9/11; casualties could run into the millions. Since the early 1990s, trying to prevent such attacks has become a major element of international efforts to prevent and combat terrorism.

Yet how serious is the threat? How likely is it that terrorist groups will be able to acquire and deploy WMDs? Are some groups more dangerous in this regard than others? The Algerian case is a clear warning that terrorist groups are active on this front, though the result is as much a clear warning to them that CBRN weapons are far from easy to make or deploy. Fictional plots centred around terrorists using one or more of such weapons have been a staple of the film and television industry for decades, but real life has tended to provide us with very few examples. The START Global Terrorism Database records information on nearly 100,000 terrorist incidents between 1970 and 2010. Of these, just 229 incidents involved the use of chemical, biological or radiological weapons; no incident has involved nuclear weapons to date. A closer examination of the cases shows that it would be a serious mistake to view them all as potential cases of WMD terrorism. For example, many of the incidents involved the use of tear gas canisters. This was enough for the incident to qualify as an act of chemical terrorism, even though the tear gas was not lethal and the terrorists used other weapons (usually guns and explosives) to do the real harm in the attack. This is a recurring theme in many of the cases. Usually the CBR element played a surprisingly minor role and conventional weapons were the ones which actually killed people.

Attacks where the CBR weapons are the ones that do kill are very rare – only 24 incidents in 40 years. The best-known cases are the 1995 Tokyo subway attack and the 2001 anthrax letters in the US. Together with the other incidents, they demonstrate that CBRN attacks *can* happen, albeit rarely. Such attacks, however, have *never* caused mass fatalities, and the popular acronym 'weapons of mass destruction' in describing CBRN weapons is desperately misleading – at least with regard to terrorism.

Despite the rarity of past CBRN attacks and the extreme unlikelihood of terrorists being able to accomplish a truly devastating attack using these weapons, CBRN attack remains a popular topic for government and funding bodies. They will award funding and resources for work in this area when other far more common and consistently more deadly terrorist tactics are ignored. Those who hoped that 9/11 – a stunning example of how non-CBRN weapons can be used to kill thousands of people – might have heralded at least a modest shift away from a CBRN obsession have been disappointed.

Nevertheless, public expectation remains high that sooner or later serious attacks will be carried out by terrorists using CBRN weapons. As early as 1998, President Clinton stated that he believed a terrorist attack using chemical or biological weapons would be mounted against a US city within five years. Three years later, in 2001, he was proved correct when seven letters containing anthrax were mailed to targets in Miami and Washington, D.C., killing five people and infecting 22. The economic cost of decontaminating the affected sites was estimated at around $320 million. The perpetrator of the anthrax attacks was never fully determined, although there were strong indications that the attack had been carried out by a disgruntled US scientist who had access to weapons grade anthrax.

Even before 2001, the US government had vastly increased the funding available for WMD terrorism. In 1999, $2.8 billion was spent on preparations for an expected catastrophic attack (at the same time, funding for dealing with groups such as Al-Qaeda was reduced or curtailed). The impetus for this concentration of American concern on WMD terrorism stemmed primarily from the Tokyo subway attack in 1995, which left 12 people dead and 5,500 injured. For many, the Tokyo sarin attack was a wake-up call to the world's large cities, a warning of just how vulnerable they are to attacks by terrorists who are prepared to use such weapons.

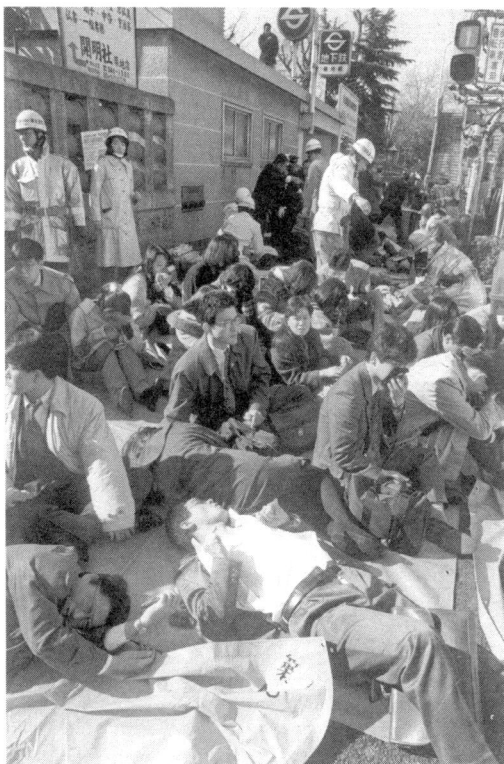

▲ The aftermath of the 1995 Tokyo sarin attack.

It is generally agreed by most analysts that terrorist groups are unlikely to acquire a nuclear device in the near future. To begin with, it is very doubtful that a terrorist group will ever be able to manufacture its own nuclear device. The suggestion that a small team of suitably qualified scientists in a well-stocked modern laboratory would be able to come up with a nuclear bomb is simply fiction. If it were really that easy, countries such as Iran would have acquired a nuclear capability long ago. Instead, after spending billions of dollars funding the work of thousands of scientists and technicians, that country has yet to be successful. Dictatorships in Iraq and Libya also failed to develop such weapons despite heavy investment, and those countries which have succeeded – such as Pakistan, Israel, India and North Korea – did so only after extraordinary expense and effort. DIY atomics is simply not a feasible option for terrorist groups with their limited resources.

A greater risk is the possibility that a terrorist might get his hands on a nuclear weapon made by someone else. Early in the 1990s, a Bosnian politician was discovered with a large quantity of nuclear material in his possession. What he intended to do with it is uncertain, but the discovery sent a wave of anxiety through Western security services. The Bosnian material had been smuggled out of Russia, and the constant fear throughout the 1990s and into the 2000s was that eventually some of the former Soviet Union's vast nuclear stockpile would fall into the wrong hands. However, while small amounts of radioactive material have been smuggled out of Russia since 1990, security sources do not believe that a nuclear warhead or explosive device has yet been acquired.

Much greater fear surrounds the possibility of biological and chemical weapons. It is generally agreed that it would be far easier for a terrorist group to develop weapons of this sort. The terrorist attacks mounted by the religious cult Aum Shinrikyo provide a frightening example. Most people are aware of the Tokyo subway attack in 1995, but few realize that this was just one of at least 12 attacks using chemical and biological weapons which were carried out by the cult. Aum Shinrikyo first began its terrorist campaign in 1990. Initially the group focused on developing biological weapons, including botulism and anthrax, and they made a serious attempt to obtain the deadly Ebola virus. In 1990 the group developed a botulin gas and sent three trucks filled with the mix to selected targets in Japan (including a US military base). The gas was released but had no effect whatsoever, and to the intense frustration of the group the entire incident went unnoticed by both the media and the authorities. Later, the cult mounted two large-scale attacks using anthrax in Tokyo, but incredibly no one became ill or died as a result. There was also an attempt to contaminate the Japanese parliament, but despite spraying the entrance of the parliament building with what should have been a catastrophic dose of botulin gas, yet again not a single individual was infected.

Not surprisingly, Aum Shinrikyo eventually decided that biological weapons were simply too ineffective and turned their hand instead to chemical weapons. The cult focused on producing the deadly nerve gas sarin, but early attempts to use the weapon either failed or backfired, with the death of a cult member. The group's scientists struggled to develop the right mix and also struggled to find an effective way to disperse the gas.

In an attempt to derail a court case against the cult, in 1994 activists mounted a night-time attack, spraying sarin over a building in an effort to kill the three judges presiding over the case. The judges were injured in the attack and a shift in wind meant that people sleeping in nearby apartments were also seriously affected. Seven died and more than 250 were injured.

For the Tokyo subway attack the following year, Aum tried but failed to develop a sophisticated way to disperse the sarin. In the end, the attackers were reduced to almost pathetic measures – using the sharpened ends of umbrellas to punch through plastic containers containing a liquid form of sarin. Although 12 died, the diluted sarin and crude dispersal methods meant that overall the toll was far less than it might have been.

While these episodes may seem like a litany of incompetence on the part of Aum Shinrikyo, nothing could be further from the truth. As terrorist groups go, the cult was superbly equipped. The group commanded financial resources in excess of $1 billion. They had a dedicated team of nearly 300 highly qualified scientists working on their weapons projects, and some activists had received extensive training from members of elite Russian military units. A 2007 assessment concluded that Aum was 'the most technologically innovative terrorist organization in history'. While chemical and biological weapons are in theory capable of inflicting mass casualties, the harsh reality Aum Shinrikyo encountered is that such weapons are incredibly difficult to use in the real world. Supposedly lethal viruses and bacteria simply did not infect and kill people when they were released. Chemicals were somewhat more effective. However, they were extremely dangerous to develop and deploy, and the effect was quite limited. The quantity of sarin used in the Tokyo attack was theoretically capable of killing 50,000 adults. Yet on the day, just 12 died.

The day of super terrorism has not yet arrived. Tokyo was an early warning sign, an indication of what may come. The anthrax attacks in 2001 represented another warning – though this was far from being a typical terrorist plot and the circumstances which led to that attack are unlikely to recur frequently. The vast sums spent on this area over the past 20 years, however, is almost certainly excessive and an overreaction. In the eight years after the 2001 anthrax attacks, the US government alone spent over $50 billion to try to address the threat of biological weapons. Serious questions need to be asked about whether this was a sensible expenditure and a realistic response to the threat.

For terrorists, nuclear, radiological, chemical and biological weapons are currently too expensive and too dangerous for all but the very richest groups to contemplate using them effectively. The authorities often argue that groups such as Aum Shinrikyo provided other terrorist organizations with a model of the impact super terrorism can have. That is true. But Aum Shinrikyo also showed the other groups just how expensive and difficult weapons of mass destruction are to acquire and, even more importantly, how incredibly difficult it is to use them; 85 per cent of Aum Shinrikyo's WMD attacks killed or injured no one apart from their own members. The disastrous experience of AQLIM in 2009 only reinforces that point. These are the pragmatic lessons that most terrorist groups observe. They also note, however, the massive media attention surrounding the rare successful attacks, and that will act as an incentive for some groups to continue considering acts of super terrorism.

Will we see more terrorist attacks using such weapons? Yes. The key question is whether terrorist groups will ever be able to cross the threshold of being able to efficiently produce and deploy such weapons. Aum Shinrikyo managed to get halfway there; they could produce the weapons but they could not work out how to use them effectively. Inevitably, other terrorist groups will try to learn from those failures.

**8**

# Countering
# terrorism

*One does not use a tank to catch field
mice – a cat will do the job better.*

*George Grivas-Dighenis, EOKA commander*

ALL THAT
MATTERS

Given how weak they are compared to the governments they are fighting, it is incredible how hard it is to defeat some terrorist groups. Even at its height, Al-Qaeda as a movement enjoyed a budget of probably no more than tens of millions of US dollars per year and an active membership of a few thousand. (The amount of his wealth that Osama bin Laden was able to pour into the movement has generally been grossly overestimated.) This was the group that decided to declare war on the planet's only superpower and its allies. In the 1990s, when Al-Qaeda started to stir the American giant, the US government typically spent over $1.5 trillion each year, $300 billion of this going to its military and $26 billion to its intelligence agencies. Over 1.4 million well-trained, disciplined volunteers staffed its armed forces, using weapons and equipment which enjoyed decisive technological advantages over that of the rest of the world's military forces.

▲ Following the 9/11 attacks, the US found itself embroiled in an expensive and lingering global war on terror. More than a decade on, the fighting continues.

So how is it that, having awakened this giant, Al-Qaeda is still with us? Not only with us but, incredibly, still the number one international terrorist threat? Hundreds of thousands of people have been killed in the global war on terror deliberately provoked by Al-Qaeda. Countries have been invaded, regimes toppled, great quantities of blood and treasure spilt in a series of seemingly relentless conflicts in various troubled corners of the world. Yet Al-Qaeda has survived, battered, yes, but still in the game.

The American experience with Al-Qaeda is not unique. About 10 per cent of terrorist groups go on to win their conflicts – a sobering statistic given the number of groups and the paltry resources at their disposal when most conflicts start. Yet the successes of terrorist groups in these struggles usually tell us more about the inept responses of the governments opposing them than the creativity and skill of the terrorists. Terrorism is a contest in blunders. Terrorists need governments to make mistakes if they are to thrive, and all too often governments seem willing to oblige.

At a fundamental level, almost all terrorist campaigns want to:

▶ provoke the state into taking aggressive and rash actions

▶ escalate the nature and extent of the violence in the conflict

▶ convince onlookers that the government is to blame for the violence

▶ outlast the government's willingness to sustain the struggle.

In order for counter-terrorism to be effective, it needs to keep a firm eye on this linked chain and to constantly bear in mind what it is that the terrorists are trying to achieve at each step.

States respond in a range of ways. Traditionally, governments initially attempt to deal with the conflict using existing measures for exerting order and control, often relying on the criminal justice system. Frequently these prove adequate to the situation and the threat is eliminated or reduced to an acceptable level. When the threat is more prolonged, or there has been an especially provocative attack, the state faces greater challenges in determining how best to respond.

Governments usually pursue a range of different aims when they fight terrorism, though it is relatively rare for these aims to be clearly articulated or carefully co-ordinated. Indeed, governments themselves frequently lack a sophisticated and clear understanding of exactly what they are trying to achieve and how they are going to do it. Specific policies might include trying to:

◗ deter terrorists and their supporters by introducing severe penalties and punishments

◗ increase the ability of the security forces to identify, disrupt and incapacitate terrorists

◗ reduce the vulnerability of potential targets

◗ address symbolic needs, e.g. being seen to share public revulsion/outrage at an event

◗ tackle underlying grievances and root causes.

Usually a combination of aims will be operating at any one time and the relative priority placed on any one is not constant. Some objectives can be abandoned, others resurrected. As a result, the overall counter-terrorism strategy can turn out to be a confused mix of initiatives and practices, with some elements jarring against and even sabotaging others. Often this confusion is unintentional. At other times, it reflects rivalries and tensions within the state's structures and systems. Sometimes it simply reflects the harsh consequence of bigger priorities overshadowing the counter-terrorism arena.

Not having a clear game plan of what it is you are trying to achieve is a recipe for disaster. In recent years one of the best examples of a clearly designed counter-terrorism strategy is the UK's CONTEST strategy. This was first introduced in 2003 and an updated version was added in 2009, although the main principles remain unchanged. CONTEST focuses not only on identifying and apprehending active terrorists but also on tackling the root causes of extremism in order to deprive terrorist groups of recruits and support from communities. The strategy also focuses attention on protecting critical infrastructure. Finally, there is an acknowledgement that terrorist attacks may still occur despite all agencies' best efforts, and as a result the strategy incorporates an important resilience strand. This is intended to ensure that there will be a capable emergency response if a terrorist attack occurs and that society will be able to continue to work effectively in the aftermath.

On paper, a system like CONTEST makes a great deal of sense – it tries to incorporate a range of different aims in a cohesive framework and to deal with the threat in a holistic manner. In practice, of course, it has run into a series of problems, especially around the so-called Prevent strand aimed at tackling root causes and preventing radicalization.

Some root causes are not simply inconvenient truths, they are political untouchables. After the CONTEST strategy was first introduced, for several years British governments claimed that the nation's foreign policy was not a root cause of jihadi terrorism in the UK. This issue revolved around the fallout from the UK's involvement in the conflicts in Iraq and Afghanistan. There was overwhelming evidence that this involvement *was* contributing to domestic terrorism. However, as the government was not prepared to change the overseas deployment, it brazenly argued that Iraq and Afghanistan played no part in radicalization.

It was an absurd argument, but the UK is far from alone in pushing absurd arguments when talking about terrorism. In public, many states deliberately downplay some factors or even officially deny that they play any role whatsoever in a conflict. Naturally this makes a mockery of serious efforts to tackle the root causes, and the governments know this.

Which leads us to a vital point that is often overlooked in public debates on counter-terrorism. Put bluntly, most of the time terrorism is not the most serious problem a state faces (in the West or elsewhere). Even for states embroiled in a relatively serious terrorist conflict, terrorism generally is not among the top five challenges the state is facing (although politicians will usually not admit this in public).

This has consequences.

While terrorism might get a lot of media attention, the amount of harm it causes in the grand scheme of things is usually very limited. As a result, the incentive for a state – any state – to invest massive resources and prolonged effort purely to counter terrorism will normally be very limited. In the aftermath of a particularly atrocious attack, resources may temporarily be thrown at the problem, but this will usually be a short-lived move, and often is more about style than substance.

Further, many regimes may be willing to endorse and engage in policies which are known to be ineffective – or even counter-productive – in dealing with terrorism simply because the benefits of such policies in other spheres are considered to be of more strategic importance.

This helps to explain the many cases where apparently intelligent, well-educated politicians – surrounded by even smarter and better-educated advisors – make such obviously bad policy decisions in terms of fighting terrorism. The decision-makers often have a good understanding that the policy won't work – and that it may even make the problem worse – but the gains in other arenas, usually resolving around economics and domestic and international politics, are judged worth the cost. It is not that the government does not care about terrorism, it is just that it cares about other factors *more*.

For the terrorist, of course, this represents an opportunity. The terrorists' primary objective is to win the conflict it is fighting against the state. The government's primary objectives are much more byzantine, especially in the opening phases of a conflict. At this early stage, defeating a particular terrorist group might not even rank in the state's top 50 aims. Indeed, usually it will not be until the terrorist group has extensively mobilized and is engaged in widespread and serious violence that the state finally makes defeating it a major priority.

Having to juggle a range of priorities is complicated even further for governments by the fact that the easy and popular options are often also the most useless and unhelpful. Terrorism, itself the extreme use of violence and force, encourages a view that forceful and violent responses are not only justified in combating it but are also obligatory. For example, in 1968 the IRA was a moribund, shrivelled and irrelevant organization. How, in the space of a handful of years, could this near-defunct group turn into the largest, best-equipped, best-funded terrorist organization in the Western world? A major factor in the growth of the IRA was not the skill and acumen of its leaders and members, but the ineptitude of the manner in which the state chose to subdue it. It was only when crude and oppressive security policies gave many previously uninvolved Catholics ample reason to hate the police and the British army that the recruits began joining up en masse.

One of the many policies which alienated the local community were the destructive house searches carried out by the security forces. In the search for weapons and other contraband, each home was effectively wrecked. Carpets and floorboards were pulled up, doors kicked in, furniture destroyed, walls and ceilings knocked open with drills and sledgehammers. This was first witnessed on a large scale during the Falls Road curfew of July 1970, when, in the space of three days, thousands of Catholic houses in west Belfast were aggressively searched by 3,000 soldiers, who also temporarily sealed off the district from the rest of the city. During 1971, 50 Catholic homes were raided every day – almost 18,000 houses over the course of the year – directly impacting on over 100,000 Catholics. In a two-month period, out of nearly 1,200 homes 'searched' in this manner, weapons were found in just 47 cases.

These trends continued throughout the early 1970s, the IRA provoking the security services, which generally lacked the restraint necessary to win the propaganda war. By the end of 1970, IRA membership had grown from 100 to over 800 in Belfast alone. In an attempt to control the burgeoning growth, internment without trial was introduced in August 1971. Internment was meant to allow the imprisonment of IRA activists quickly and efficiently. In reality, internment was the biggest miscalculation made in an attempt to end the violence. The intelligence on which people were detained was often appallingly poor. Most of those arrested were released without charge after humiliating interrogations (in some cases involving torture), for the innocent a deeply unpleasant, offensive and bitter encounter with the security forces. In its wake and for as long as it continued, IRA recruitment soared. The killing of 13 people on 30 January 1972

('Bloody Sunday') by British paratroopers in Derry added further to the vilification of the security forces. A 14th victim died later in hospital. Such atrocities did much to cement international sympathy for the IRA, particularly in the USA. Strong local support, ample manpower, newly acquired funds and weapons allowed the IRA to conduct an unprecedented campaign of violence against the police, judiciary and army. The destruction and death toll escalated dramatically, with one major consequence being the disbanding of the province's regional government.

Yet in polls and surveys carried out in the aftermath of terrorist attacks, a clear majority consistently voice approval for their government to take tough action and in particular to use military force against terrorism. Though widely condemned internationally, the American strike against Libya in 1986 was approved by 77 per cent of the US citizens polled. The two strikes authorized by the Clinton administration, first against Iraq in 1993 and then against Al-Qaeda in 1998, had approval ratings of 66 and 77 per cent respectively, even though the latter occurred at a time when the president himself was embroiled in a humiliating personal scandal. After the terrorist attacks on 11 September 2001, the use of military force in Afghanistan received massive domestic support, with 87 per cent of Americans expressing approval. Today, the highly controversial campaign of drone strikes also remains consistently popular within the US.

As the survey and poll results stress, for any government that wishes to make a widely popular response to terrorist violence (at least among its own population), tough, aggressive actions are by far the most obvious choice.

Their popularity gives the politicians and leaders who authorise them wider support, and the short-term results provide the security forces with evidence of apparent success: terrorists disabled, weapons and resources confiscated, operations and networks disrupted.

However there is a serious downside. When the British introduced harsh measures to tackle the IRA, recruits and support flooded to the organization. When the US bombed Libya, the Libyans increased their involvement and buttressing of terrorism rather than pulling away from it. When Israel kills Hamas members and imposes other sanctions on Palestinian communities, they increase the sense of perceived injustice – particularly considering the often high loss of innocent life – driving more recruits into extremist groups and facilitating increased sympathy and support for these groups not only within the West Bank and Gaza but also among the international community. As a result, Israel and other governments may win skirmish after skirmish but still find themselves unable to establish lasting peace and stability until other counter-terrorism policies are given greater priority and prominence. The outlook is hardly encouraging for the US, still aggressively hunting down Al-Qaeda and its affiliates throughout the world, yet it may find that a lasting resolution to the pursuit eludes it, regardless of how much energy and military force it invests in the campaign.

# 9

# The future

*Remember, we have only to be lucky once. You will have to be lucky always.*

*IRA statement claiming responsibility for the
1984 Brighton bombing*

ALL THAT
MATTERS

Terrorism comes in waves. In the past 150 years, four great waves of terrorist violence have spread across the globe. The first wave struck in the 1870s with the rise of anarchist revolutionaries, initially appearing in Russia but then rapidly spreading throughout Europe and beyond. This was eventually eclipsed by a wave of nationalist terrorism in the aftermath of the First World War. The advent of the Cold War between the West and Communism brought with it the third wave of left-wing inspired terrorism, often sponsored by Soviet nations. Finally, as the Cold War itself ended, the fourth wave emerged – religiously motivated terrorism – and we are still living within its shadow.

On average each wave has lasted 40 years. They rise, peak and eventually recede. Some groups persist beyond the demise of the wave which spawned them, but it is generally clear to observers that an overall shift has taken place and that terrorism's centre of gravity has shifted elsewhere.

With such a history, a key question for many is what form will the next wave take?

It is possible that the current religious wave has peaked and may have already entered a decline phase. That perhaps might be a little optimistic, but one certainty is that the religious wave *will* decline at some point. While the wave will recede, some religiously motivated groups will doubtless persist throughout the 21st century – we may well still be facing Al-Qaeda or its direct descendent at the dawn of the next century. That said, it is not inevitable that religiously motivated groups will dominate the rest of the 21st century in the same way that they have dominated its opening decade.

*The future*

Terrorism does not stand apart from the wider world. The great waves have all been closely tied to major geopolitical world events and processes. The anarchists were born out of the rise of the middle classes, the spread of education and the growing intolerance of autocratic rule in the 19th century. The nationalists were inextricably linked to the collapse of the great European colonial empires which started to crumble in the slaughter of the First World War, and which would take nearly 40 more years to be dismantled. The third wave followed the spread of the Communist states in the aftermath of the USSR's victory in the Second World War. In the Cold War nuclear stalemate, terrorism became a useful proxy for states who could no longer dare to grapple directly.

The eventual collapse of the Soviet empire brought that wave to an end and accelerated the rise of religiously motivated terrorism. Globalization increasingly brought a secular and individualistic Western culture into convulsive conflict with more traditional, community-focused, religious ones. The clash crystallized most obviously in the collision between secularism and conservative Islam, although extremist elements of most major religions have been involved to some degree. In recent decades almost all of the most serious acts of terrorism have emerged (directly or indirectly) from this clash between secularism and belief.

Throughout the different waves, terrorism has been a by-product of bigger forces. Sometimes the rise of terrorism has been deliberate and intentional. Often it has been accidental and unanticipated.

Looking ahead, the key question is not what form will terrorism take in the future, but rather what will be the major global processes driving the new waves of terrorism? What are the international forces and events which will ignite and stir terrorist conflicts in their wake? If we can anticipate what these might be, we will be in a far better position to understand the future of terrorism.

Four trends stand out as a cause for concern. First, the world's population is increasing. Population size alone is the best predictor we have for the eruption of terrorism. As the world's population increases further, the risks overall go up. The current world population stands at over 7 billion, but by 2050 it will be over 9 billion. The shift away from rural living to urban environments is also accelerating; more than 60 per cent of people will live in cities and towns in the coming decades. Added to this, many societies are forecast to experience massive youth bulges – as their population increases, there will also be a particularly huge rise in those aged between 15 and 30. Experience shows that societies with such youth bulges are especially prone to social unrest and civil strife, and we are already beginning to witness their emergence in critical regions such as Saudi Arabia and Yemen.

Added to an overall increase in population is another major trend, increased global migration. This is being driven by a range of factors, not least of which is the growing impact of global warming. Fresh patterns of migration are anticipated in the coming decades, with the developed world remaining the most popular target for many migrant groups. Inevitably, the increase in global migration is going to lead to a major increase in diaspora communities in the host countries. Should these diasporas fail to integrate successfully in their host societies – and some inevitably will struggle – this could give rise to new ethnic tensions and extremism as well as adding fresh impetus to some older veins.

The next generally accepted future trend of concern is the declining strength of the United States of America. The 20th century was the American century. The US may end the 21st century still technically the world's most powerful state, but the gap between the US and rival powers is shrinking significantly and may vanish entirely. In economic terms, this decline has been unfolding for several decades already, but fading economic might will inevitably be followed by the US gradually losing its military superiority over its closest rivals. Initially, the rivals will gain parity in only narrow, specific niches, but gradually these will spread as the century progresses.

With declining economic strength and an eroding military edge, American foreign policy in the 21st century will be transformed and ultimately will be radically different from what we have seen over the last 70 years. At the very least, by the middle of the 21st century America will probably no longer be capable of launching a global war on terror as it did in the aftermath of 9/11.

That said, it is unlikely that the USA will be eclipsed by a new global superpower (despite the frequent rhetoric about China). Rather, there will be a levelling of the playing field, with the emergence of a small number of states which enjoy comparatively similar levels of economic and military power. Each of these states will exert tremendous control and influence within their own regions, and they are unlikely to be seriously challenged in those local arenas by the other powers.

▲ Rising global populations and intensifying competition for resources are likely to feed the terrorist conflicts of the coming century.

Where fierce challenges will occur, however, is over the control of natural resources, and this is the fourth critical trend of the 21st century. As economies outside the West continue to grow, they are becoming increasingly resource-hungry and competition to sustain supplies is intensifying. China and India are the two stand-out economies in this regard, but others such as Brazil are also becoming formidable. Meanwhile, demand in the West shows no sign of slackening, and as overall competition intensifies, the potential for conflict – and especially low-level proxy conflicts – will escalate. The clashes may focus more on establishing and protecting friendly regimes in supplier nations than on direct confrontations with other major players. As a result, some supplier nations – especially those in Africa, the Middle East and Latin America – may become increasingly vulnerable to destabilization and internal conflict.

# ▶ Final thoughts

Terrorism will be with us for a very long time to come. In the aftermath of terrorist attacks – and especially those with heavy casualties – it is often incredibly difficult to engage in objective analysis of the causes and processes leading to the event. Instead governments, analysts and the wider public can become obsessed with response and punishment. The terrorists are demonized, stripped of their humanity, and assumed to be callous fanatics delighting in the carnage they have created and against whom the most extreme measures are appropriate and justified. Those who suggest otherwise are dismissed as sympathisers or appeasers. Yet terrorism is not a simple phenomenon; on the contrary it is highly complex. Worse, it is a highly complex problem whose understanding is undermined and corrupted by a cabal of virulent myths and half-truths whose reach extends even to the most learned and experienced.

In the end, organized and planned campaigns of violence do not happen within a vacuum and they are not driven by trivial or fleeting motivations which reside in and are shared only by the perpetrators. Terrorism is not the work of madmen or devils, and to try to get to grips with it in those terms is to fight it with a very mistaken concept of who one's enemies are and how and why they are supported.

Any act of terrorist violence will defy simple explanation. The temptation to view it wholly as a manifestation of evil is understandable but ill-judged. Such a view provides no practical insight, no understanding of the circumstances and processes which produced the act, and no true insight into the perpetrators and their supporters. Thus one is no better prepared or placed to prevent similar acts of violence in the future.

Embracing the caricatures which often pass as explanations for the causes of terrorism facilitates only embracing the caricatures which pass for effective responses. Amid the carnage and rubble of atrocity we must not allow or encourage the luxury of a simple and demonized foe. This is not an elementary struggle to be easily dismissed: rather it is complex, evolving and sometimes terribly resilient. Lasting solutions and lasting safety will not be found until our understanding matches far more closely our horror.

# Ten key terrorist attacks

**1.** Sarajevo, 1914. The most important terrorist event in history involved the deaths of just two people. On 28 June 1914, a 19-year-old extremist, Gavrilo Princip, shot and killed the heir to the Austro-Hungarian Empire, Archduke Franz Ferdinand, and his wife while they were visiting Sarajevo. Princip was one of a group of Black Hand terrorists in the city that day to assassinate the Archduke. Sponsored by the Serbian military, Black Hand was motivated by Slavic nationalism. The killings acted as the direct catalyst for the start of the First World War six weeks later. That conflict laid the foundations of almost every other major war of the 20th century. Even now, a century later, we have still not entirely escaped the shadow of Princip's actions.

**2.** 9/11, 2001. On 11 September 2001, 19 terrorists belonging to Al-Qaeda hijacked four passenger jets shortly after take-off in the United States. The hijackers used the planes to carry out kamikaze attacks against the World Trade Center in New York and the US military's headquarters building at the Pentagon in Washington D.C. The fourth plane crashed into a field in Pennsylvania but was believed to have been intended for a high-profile target in Washington D.C. Almost 3,000 people were killed in the attacks – the highest loss of life ever suffered directly in a terrorist attack. The attacks led immediately to the US-led war on terror which dominated international politics over the following decade and which, in different forms, still continues.

**100 IDEAS**

3. **Munich Olympics, 1972.** On 5 September 1972, eight terrorists belonging to Black September stormed the Israeli team accommodation in the Olympic Village, killing two people and taking a further nine hostage. After several hours of negotiations, the authorities agreed to provide a passenger jet to fly the terrorists and their hostages out of the country. A botched attempt was made to overpower the terrorists at the airport which resulted in the deaths of all the hostages and one policeman. All of the terrorists were killed or captured. Nine hundred million people in at least 100 countries witnessed the event live on television as the crisis unfolded. Black September claimed one week later that: 'The choice of the Olympics, from the purely propagandistic viewpoint, was 100 per cent successful. It was like painting the name of Palestine on a mountain that can be seen from the four corners of the earth.'

4. **Killing of Tsar Alexander II, St Petersburg, 1881.** On 13 March 1881, terrorists belonging to Narodnaya Volya assassinated the emperor of Russia, Tsar Alexander II. The terrorists were fighting to reform the autocratic Russian state, but, ironically, killing the tsar utterly destroyed the democratic reform process which had begun during Alexander's reign. His successor returned Russia to an even more dictatorial state, exacerbating Russia's growing internal social, economic and political problems, and contributing significantly to the rise of Bolshevism in the following decades, with major international consequences.

5. **Tokyo sarin attack, 1995.** The Tokyo subway attack carried out by the religious cult Aum Shinrikyo in 1995 remains the most serious use of CBRN (chemical, biological, radiological, nuclear) weapons by terrorists to date. Twelve people were killed and over 1,000 injured (with many more psychological casualties). Widely seen as a watershed moment in the threat posed by

terrorism, it also highlighted the huge problems in using such weapons. The attackers were reduced to using the sharpened ends of umbrellas to punch through plastic containers containing liquid sarin. Although in theory there was enough sarin to kill 50,000 people, the diluted chemicals and poor dispersal methods meant that the impact was massively reduced.

6. **US Marine barracks, Beirut, 1983.** On 23 October 1983, a suicide bomber connected with a group that would become *Hezbollah*, used a truck bomb to attack the US Marine barracks at Beirut airport, killing 241 American military personnel. It was one of the heaviest losses of life that the US military had suffered in a single day since the Second World War. The bombing was one of a series of suicide attacks in the region which effectively marked the beginning of the modern age of suicide terrorism. Within four months of the bombing, US military forces pulled out of Lebanon and did not return.

7. **King David Hotel, Jerusalem, 1946.** On 22 July 1946, a huge bomb detonated in the King David Hotel in Jerusalem, killing 91 people and injuring 46. This was the most lethal terrorist bombing up to this date. The hotel contained the administrative and military headquarters for the British authorities in Palestine. It was targeted by the terrorist group Irgun, which wanted to drive the British out of the region. Britain pulled out the following year and the State of Israel was created by the United Nations General Assembly on 29 November 1947.

8. **Bishopsgate bombing, London, 1993.** On 24 April 1993, the IRA used a truck to carry a 2,300lb fertilizer bomb into Bishopsgate in the financial heart of London (the equivalent of Wall Street in New York). The resulting blast caused damage approaching $2 billion to buildings housing prestigious foreign and domestic banks and other financial organizations. The impact was so severe

that it brought about a crisis in the insurance industry and led to the near collapse of Lloyds of London. The IRA had telephoned a coded warning before the detonation so the area had largely been evacuated, but even so one person was killed and over 60 injured. It was the most economically devastating attack ever carried out by the group and illustrated how attacks could still have a massive impact even when casualties are low.

9. **Customs House attack, Dublin, 1921.** Winning terrorist conflicts is more about perception than anything else. On 25 May 1921, approximately 130 members of the IRA carried out a large-scale attack against Customs House in Dublin. This huge building was the administrative centre of British government in Ireland and also the primary location for all Irish tax records. The IRA took control of the building and set it ablaze. The building was destroyed but nearly 90 IRA members were killed, captured or wounded before they could escape. Like the Tet Offensive in Vietnam, the attack was technically a military disaster but was nevertheless a spectacular propaganda success. It created a powerful impression that the IRA were far from beaten in the conflict. It added significantly to the impetus in London to reach a negotiated settlement with the Irish nationalists. Within seven weeks a lasting cease-fire was declared.

10. **Pan Am flight 103, 1988.** On 21 December 1988, a bomb brought down the passenger jet Pan Am flight 103 over the town of Lockerbie in Scotland. All 259 people on board were killed, along with 11 people on the ground. It remains the most lethal act of terrorism ever to occur in the UK. Suspicion fell initially on Iran as the sponsors for the attack (in retaliation for the shooting down of an Iranian passenger jet by an American ship). However, attention soon switched to Libya and a Libyan intelligence agent, Abdelbaset al-Megrahi, was ultimately convicted and imprisoned for the bombing. The motivation was

believed to be retaliation for the American bombings of Libya in 1986, in one of which a young daughter of Libya's ruler, Muammar Qaddafi, was killed.

# Ten key terrorists

11. Osama bin Laden (1957–2011): founder and long-term leader of Al-Qaeda. Born into an extremely wealthy Saudi family, bin Laden travelled to Afghanistan during the Soviet conflict and laid the foundations there for Al-Qaeda. Following the Iraq invasion of Kuwait in 1990, he offered to help the Saudi authorities but they chose instead to accept a powerful US military presence in the country. Attacks by Al-Qaeda against US targets in the 1990s were primarily a reaction to the continued US presence in Saudi Arabia. Before 9/11, bin Laden was already at the top of the FBI's most wanted list. After the 2001 attacks, the US launched and sustained a major effort to crush Al-Qaeda and capture or kill him. He eluded capture for many years until finally, in 2011, he was tracked down to a compound in Pakistan where he was killed in a raid by US special forces.

12. Illich Ramirez Sanchez (1949– ). Better known as 'Carlos the Jackal', he was born in Venezuela and inherited his father's Marxist leanings. In 1969 he joined the Popular Front for the Liberation of Palestine (PFLP) and received training from them in Jordan. He carried out several attacks in Europe in collaboration with a variety of terrorist groups. In December 1975 he led the terrorist consortium which killed three people and took hostage 11 OPEC oil ministers in Vienna and successfully obtained $50 million in ransom for their safe release. Following this event, which cemented his international celebrity, he increasingly became a gun-for-hire rather than an activist guided by a clear political philosophy. He was based mainly in Eastern Europe and the Middle East,

but seemed to have a knack for alienating his hosts. In 1994, Sudan extradited him to France, where he remains in prison.

13. Patricia Hearst (1954– ): one of the most remarkable terrorists in history. Daughter of the millionaire publisher William Randolph Hearst, she was kidnapped in 1974 by the Symbionese Liberation Army (SLA). After two months of captivity she sent an incredible message claiming she had decided to join the group. For over two years she remained with the SLA, taking part in at least one bank robbery. Eventually she was captured/rescued by the FBI, but despite being free from the threat or influence of the SLA, she continued to espouse their political beliefs. Her case came to be regarded as a classic example of Stockholm Syndrome, which leads hostages to start to identify and sympathise strongly with those holding them hostage.

14. Michael Collins (1890–1922). One of the most effective terrorist leaders of the 20th century, Collins spearheaded the IRA's campaign against British forces in Ireland between 1919 and 1921. A charismatic leader, he recognized the crucial importance of winning the intelligence war and was able to seriously undermine British efforts through a combination of public support, double agents, infiltration, intimidation and assassination. He was part of the Irish delegation to the treaty negotiations in 1921 which ultimately ended the conflict. This resulted in the creation of an Irish Free State but with six counties of Ulster (subsequently known as Northern Ireland) remaining part of the UK. Collins led the pro-treaty forces in the civil war which followed but was killed in an ambush in its closing stages. This, though, did not prevent an ultimate pro-treaty victory.

15. Ayman al-Zawahiri (1951– ). The current leader of Al-Qaeda, he was the group's second in command for many years and was the natural successor when Osama

bin Laden was killed in 2011. Egyptian-born, he was connected with the group that assassinated the Egyptian president Anwar Sadat in 1981. He was detained in the aftermath of this assassination and was brutally tortured in Egyptian jail in the early 1980s. Upon release he became leader of Egyptian Islamic Jihad. In the 1990s he forged an alliance with Al-Qaeda and orchestrated many deadly terrorist attacks, including the Luxor massacre in 1997. The two groups merged in 1998 with bin Laden as the overall leader. After 9/11, Zawahiri increasingly became the chief spokesman for the movement.

16. **Theodore Kaczynski** (1942– ). By the time he was arrested in April 1996, Theodore Kaczynski, better known as the Unabomber, was responsible for a 17-year-long bombing campaign in the US. He carried out a total of 16 attacks which left three people dead and 23 injured. Motivated by environmental politics, Kaczynski is the classic example of a lone-actor terrorist. The investigation to catch him cost over $50 million, making it the most expensive manhunt in US history at the time. The breakthrough in the case came in September 1995 when his 35,000-word manifesto was published in national newspapers. The bomber's brother recognized similarities between phrases and ideas in the manifesto and the writings of Kaczynski. The authorities were contacted and shortly afterwards he was arrested.

17. **Ernesto 'Che' Guevara** (1928–67). Few terrorists, if any, can match Che Guevara's lasting iconic legacy – his image is as recognizable today as when he died in 1967. As an Argentine medical student, he famously travelled across Latin America on a motorcycle. Horrified by the corruption and poverty he encountered, he eventually became a committed Marxist convinced of the necessity of revolution. A charismatic leader and insightful theorist, he played a leading role in the Cuban revolution and later

attempted to export revolution overseas. He was killed in Bolivia after being captured by government forces.

**18.** Timothy McVeigh (1968–2001). The bombing of the Murrah building in Oklahoma City in 1995 was initially suspected to be the work of foreign extremists, but the man responsible was actually a former US soldier, Timothy McVeigh. McVeigh was motivated by right-wing militia ideology and timed his attack to coincide with the second anniversary of Waco, an event he viewed as a US government massacre. McVeigh was sentenced to death for the bombing and was executed in 2001. He is often described as a lone-wolf terrorist, but this is misleading as others were also convicted for involvement in the plot.

**19.** Carlos Marighella (1911–69): a Brazilian politician who founded the terrorist group Action for National Liberation (ANL) in 1968, when he was 57 years old. He is most famous for his highly influential book, *Mini-manual of the Urban Guerrilla*, which stressed the importance of alienating local populations from the state's security forces. The most significant action of ANL was the kidnapping of the US ambassador to Brazil in 1969. The ambassador was safely released by the group following a prisoner exchange. Marighella did not live long to enjoy this success and was killed shortly afterwards in a police ambush.

**20.** Ulrike Meinhof (1934–76). One of the most famous female terrorists, she was the editor of an underground newspaper, *Konkert*, when she helped break Andreas Baader out of a West German prison in May 1970. In the aftermath, their group came to be called the Baader-Meinhof Gang and was later known as the Red Army Faction. Meinhof trained with the PLO in Jordan, and the German group co-operated with Palestinian and other militants in carrying out a series of high-profile attacks. Meinhof and most of her compatriot leaders were captured in 1972. Her psychological health deteriorated badly in prison, primarily as a result of extreme solitary confinement, and she committed suicide in May 1976.

# Eight terrorists who became national leaders

21. **Nelson Mandela** (1918–2013): widely regarded as one of the most respected statesmen of the modern era. A senior member of the African National Congress, he played a key role in convincing the movement to move from non-violent protest against the apartheid regime in South Africa to violent protest, including acts of terrorism. He helped establish the ANC's armed wing, Umkhonto we Sizwe ('Spear of the Nation'), in 1961. He spent 27 years in prison and was released in 1990. He received the Nobel Peace Prize with F. W. de Klerk in 1994 and also became president of South Africa that year after the first-ever democratic elections, stepping down in 1999 at the end of his term of office.

22. **Menachem Begin** (1913–92). He led Irgun between 1944 and 1948 in its campaign to drive the British out of Palestine and to create the state of Israel. Under his command, Irgun carried out a number of notorious attacks, including the bombing of the King David Hotel (see **Ten key terrorist attacks** above) and the abduction and hanging of two British Army sergeants in retaliation for the execution of Irgun members. He became prime minister of Israel in 1977 and played a major role in negotiating a successful peace treaty with Egypt for which both he and the Egyptian president, Anwar Sadat, were awarded the Nobel Peace Prize. He remained on Interpol's wanted list until his death in 1992.

**23.** Eamon de Valera (1882–1975). He was one of the leaders of the unsuccessful Easter Rising in Dublin in 1916 and was the most senior one not to be executed by the British in the aftermath. He was technically the overall commander of the IRA as head of the Dail in the war of independence 1919–21, though he was primarily concerned with fund-raising and propaganda activities. He led the losing anti-treaty faction in the civil war which followed, but still became the prime minister in 1932, a post he held for most of the following 25 years. Afterwards, he was elected president of Ireland from 1959 to 1973.

**24.** Ahmed Ben Bella (1916–2012). He founded two terrorist groups aimed at liberating Algeria from French control. First, in 1947 he created *Organisation Spéciale* (OS) but this had limited impact and he was jailed in 1949. He escaped in 1952, making his way to Egypt where two years later he co-founded the much more effective National Liberation Front (FLN). A bitter and intense seven-year conflict ensued. Ben Bella was captured and imprisoned again by the French in 1956, but the conflict still ended in a French defeat. He was elected Algeria's first president in 1963.

**25.** Nicos Sampson (1935–2001). He was a journalist when he joined EOKA in 1955 during that organization's struggle to force the British out of Cyprus. He used his profession as a cover to move around the country during the conflict, and claimed later that he was responsible for killing 15 British soldiers and civilians. In 1957 he was arrested and imprisoned by the British. He was released in 1960 as part of a peace deal marking the independence of Cyprus. He briefly became president of Cyprus in 1974 following a military coup.

**26.** Yasser Arafat (1929–2004). He cofounded Fatah in 1959 and used this militant group to eventually take control of the Palestinian Liberation Organization (PLO) after that was founded in 1964. The PLO's main objective was to recreate the former Arab state of Palestine and to destroy Israel. Under Arafat's leadership, Fatah and its offshoots carried out a large number of terrorist attacks in the 1960s and 1970s. Subsequently Arafat sought to increase the movement's political legitimacy, and in 1988 he publicly accepted Israel's right to exist. He became president of the Palestinian Authority in 1994 and held this post until his death in 2004. He was unable to broker a lasting peace with Israel but he largely succeeded in changing the status of the PLO from that of a terrorist organization to that of a legitimate political movement.

27. **Joseph Stalin** (1878–1953). He joined the Bolshevik party after being expelled from school and carried out a number of attacks on behalf of the party, including the notorious Tiflis bank robbery in 1907 which left 40 dead. He was arrested and imprisoned many times between 1902 and 1913, and spent time in exile in Siberia. Following Lenin's death in 1924, he outmanoeuvred his rivals and became the de facto dictator of the USSR from the late 1920s until his death. During this time approximately 15–20 million died as a result of internal repression and Sovietization policies.

28. **Pushpa Kamal Dahal** (1954– ). Dahal, better known by his *nom de guerre* 'Prachanda', led Maoist terrorists in a ten-year conflict with the monarchical government of Nepal. The conflict resulted in approximately 13,000 deaths and ended with the eventual abolition of the monarchy in 2008. Inspired by Peru's Shining Path, the Maoists nonetheless proved willing to engage in democratic elections and won a major victory in 2008 when Prachanda was elected as Nepal's prime minister.

## Two future leaders?

29. **Gerry Adams** (1948– ). He joined the IRA in the 1960s and eventually rose to a senior position in the group's ruling

Army Council. He moved increasingly into electoral politics as the president of Sinn Fein, the IRA's political wing, a position he still holds. He won a series of elections to the British Parliament (1983–92, 1997–2011) but declined to take his seat. He resigned his Westminster seat in 2011 so that he could contest a parliament seat in the Republic of Ireland, which he won. He is currently a member of the Irish parliament and has the potential to be co-leader of a future coalition government in the Republic of Ireland.

30. 'Abu Mohammad al-Julani (?– ): He is the secretive leader of Al-Nusra, one of the key groups fighting against the Bashar al-Assad regime in Syria's current civil war. Since its official emergence in 2012, Al-Nusra has been one of the most disciplined and effective fighting elements in the anti-government coalition. International unease increased, however, in the wake of apparent links with Al-Qaeda. 'Abu Mohammad al-Julani' is probably a *nom de guerre*, but if he survives the conflict, the potential for him to occupy a senior leadership role in a future Syria certainly exists.

# Key quotes about terrorism

31. 'Kill one, frighten ten thousand.' An ancient Chinese saying which captures the essence of terrorism. It is often mistakenly attributed to Sun Tzu's classic *The Art of War*.

32. 'The first maxim of your policy ought to be to lead the people by reason and the people's enemies by terror.' Maximilien Robespierre outlines the rationale for the Reign of Terror conducted by the French Revolutionary government in 1793–4.

**33.** 'They turn young men into assassins. But what can one do ... A sect cannot be destroyed by cannonballs.' Napoleon reflects on the aftermath of an assassination attempt against him on 12 October 1809. The would-be assassin, Friedrich Staps, was a young German student who wanted to rid Germany of the French presence. The emperor instructed his police minister to say that the young man was insane if talk of the assassination attempt spread.

**34.** 'We must spread our principles, not with words but with deeds, for this is the most popular, the most potent, and the most irresistible form of propaganda.' Mikhail Bakunin in 1870 provides us with the famous basis for seeing terrorism as propaganda by the deed.

**35.** 'History moves too slowly. It needs a push.' A. I. Zhelyabov, the leader of the terrorist group Narodnaya Volya, making the case for terrorism in Russia in the 1870s.

**36.** 'I am a terrorist, not a murderer.' Proud to be a terrorist, Vera Zasulich said this after shooting Governor-General Trepov in St Petersburg in 1878. Later generations of terrorists, however, would grow increasingly reluctant to use the term to describe themselves.

**37.** 'The terrorist and the policeman both come from the same basket.' A memorable line from Joseph Conrad's bleak 1907 novel *The Secret Agent*, which focused on the intrigues of anarchist terrorists in London.

**38.** 'Terror will be answered with terror.' Adolf Hitler in response to the bombing of German cities by the Allies in 1942.

**39.** 'Hatred is an element of the struggle; a relentless hatred of the enemy, impelling us over and beyond the natural limitations that man is heir to and transforming him into an effective, violent, selective and cold killing machine. Our soldiers must be thus; a people without hatred cannot vanquish a brutal enemy.' Ernesto 'Che' Guevara, the poster child of revolution, in a 1967 message shortly before his death.

**40.** 'One does not use a tank to catch field mice - a cat will do the job better.' George Grivas-Dighenis, the highly effective leader of EOKA, provides some insight into why the British military failed to defeat his small terrorist group.

**41.** 'One man's terrorist is another man's freedom fighter.' An iconic quote which captures better than any other the intractable problems of defining terrorism. It first appeared in Gerald Seymour's 1975 novel *Harry's Game*, about an undercover British agent who attempts to infiltrate the IRA.

**42.** 'Most revolutions are not caused by revolutionaries in the first place, but by the stupidity and brutality of governments.' Sean MacStiofain, the Provisional IRA's first chief of staff, draws attention to the key role the state plays in the rise of terrorism.

**43.** 'Terrorists want a lot of people watching and a lot of people listening, not a lot of people dead.' A famous quote from Brian Jenkins in 1975 which drives home the propaganda element of terrorism, even if some modern groups have grown increasingly willing to carry out mass casualty attacks.

**44.** 'Terrorism wins only if you respond to it in the way the terrorists want you to; which means that its fate is in your hands and not in theirs.' Another 1975 comment, this time from the noted historian David Fromkin, who captures an essential truth of effective counter-terrorism.

**45.** 'In order to get anywhere you have to step over a lot of dead bodies.' Ilich Ramirez Sanchez – better known as Carlos the Jackal – in typically bombastic form.

**46.** 'Remember, we have only to be lucky once. You will have to be lucky always.' IRA statement claiming responsibility for the Brighton bombing on 12 October 1984 which tried to kill the British prime minister, Margaret Thatcher, and other senior Cabinet ministers.

**47.** 'Fighting terrorism is like being a goalkeeper. You can make a hundred brilliant saves but the only shot that people remember is the one that gets past you.' A telling 1992 quote from Professor Paul Wilkinson, one of the 20th century's doyens of terrorism studies.

# Five hostage rescue successes

**48.** Entebbe airport, 1976: perhaps the most remarkable hostage rescue in history. On 27 June 1976, Air France flight 139 with over 250 passengers and crew was hijacked by a team of German and Palestinian terrorists after take-off from Athens. The flight had originated from Tel Aviv and had a large number of Jewish passengers. After refuelling in Libya, the plane landed at Uganda's Entebbe airport. Some non-Jewish hostages were released after negotiations but all the Jewish passengers were retained. On 4 July, Israel flew commandos over 2,500 miles to rescue the hostages. The commandos rapidly seized control of the airport and freed the hostages, killing six terrorists. One commando and two hostages were also killed. A third hostage, who had been moved beforehand to a nearby hospital, was later killed in retaliation for the raid.

**49.** Iranian Embassy siege, London, 1980. On 30 April 1980, six terrorists belonging to the Democratic Revolutionary Front for the Liberation of Arabistan seized control of the

Iranian Embassy in London. After five days of negotiations the terrorists shot dead one hostage and dumped his body outside the building. In response, military commandos from the SAS, the British special forces, launched a rescue mission. During a dramatic raid which was captured live on television and watched by millions, 19 hostages were freed, and five of the terrorists and one hostage were killed. The sixth terrorist was captured.

50. **Japanese Embassy siege, Lima, December 1996–April 1997.** On 17 December 1996, 14 terrorists belonging to the Tupac Amaru Revolutionary Movement (MRTA) stormed the Japanese ambassador's residence in the Peruvian capital of Lima during a diplomatic party, capturing over 500 hostages, including several foreign ambassadors as well as senior Peruvian politicians and security officials. Most hostages were released over the course of the first month, but a high-profile group of 72 were held for four months. On 22 April 1997, 125 days after the crisis began, military commandos stormed the compound and within 15 minutes two of the commandos, one hostage and all of the terrorists were killed. The success of the assault caused President Alberto Fujimori's popularity to soar from a low of 38 per cent on 15 April to a high of 65 per cent the day after the commandos were sent in.

51. **Mogadishu airport, 1977.** On 13 October 1977, four Palestinian terrorists hijacked Lufthansa flight 181 as it left Majorca with 86 passengers on board. The hijackers wanted money and the release of imprisoned terrorists. Over the ensuing days the plane travelled between international airports. In Yemen, the captain was shot dead by the terrorists; on 16 October the plane arrived at Mogadishu airport in Somalia, where it remained. The German authorities launched a rescue mission using GSG-9, a highly trained hostage-rescue team which had been set up in the aftermath of the Munich Olympics debacle. The GSG-9 commandos stormed the plane, killing three of

the terrorists and capturing the fourth. All of the hostages were freed safely. After hearing about the rescue, several imprisoned German terrorists committed suicide.

52. **Dutch hostage crisis, 1977.** On 23 May 1977, South Moluccan terrorists simultaneously seized control of a train and a school in the Netherlands. At the school, 105 children and four teachers were taken hostage, while on the train 55 passengers were seized. The terrorists wanted the release of imprisoned comrades and for previous Dutch government promises regarding an independent state to be honoured. After four days, all of the children at the school were released because they were ill (probably owing to the authorities lacing food with laxatives). After another 16 days, Dutch marines assaulted both locations. In a fierce gun battle at the train, two hostages and six terrorists were killed. All of the remaining hostages were rescued.

# Five hostage rescue disasters

53. **Beslan School siege, North Ossetia, 2004.** On 1 September 2004, a 50–70 strong group of heavily armed Chechen separatists seized control of a school in Beslan, taking hostage more than 1,200 children, teachers and parents. After three days, Russian security forces stormed the school in a chaotic and exceptionally bloody battle, which resulted in more than 331 hostages being killed, most of them children.

54. **Moscow Theatre siege, 2002.** In a pre-cursor to the 2004 Beslan attack, on 23 October 2002, 40 Chechen militants seized control of the Dubrovka theatre during a performance of the musical *Nord-Ost*. More than 900 people were taken hostage. After a stand-off lasting 57 hours, the Russian authorities pumped an anaesthetic gas into the theatre and then launched an assault. All of

the terrorists were killed in the raid – most shot in the head while unconscious – but 130 hostages also died, primarily because medical teams were not briefed on the nature of gas used and were not equipped to treat its effects.

**55. Munich, 1972.** Prior to the 1972 Olympic Games, the West German authorities had refused to believe – despite warnings – that a terrorist hostage situation was a serious threat and as a result no preparation or planning had been made to deal with one. Because of faulty intelligence and shockingly poor co-ordination and communication, not enough police were at the airport when the final rescue attempt was launched. Further, the police who were present lacked the required training and weapons. A police SWAT team that eventually did arrive was sent to the wrong part of the airport and played no part in the crisis. The resulting shoot-out was a debacle. Over a confused three-hour period, five terrorists, one police officer and all nine hostages were killed.

**56. Branch Davidian compound siege, Waco, 1993.** On 28 February 1993, Alcohol, Tobacco and Firearms (ATF) agents attempted to raid the Branch Davidian cult's compound near Waco, Texas. A fire-fight ensued which left six cult members and four ATF agents dead and 25 people injured. The FBI took control and a 51-day siege ensued. On 19 April, the FBI pumped flammable tear gas into the compound. Fires rapidly broke out, for reasons which are still contested, and 75 cult members (including 21 children) died within the compound as it burned to the ground. The incident played a major role in Timothy McVeigh's decision to bomb the Murrah building in Oklahoma in 1995.

**57. Lebanon, 2006.** On 12 July 2006, Hezbollah ambushed an Israeli military patrol on the Lebanese border with Israel, killing three soldiers and abducting two others:

Ehud Goldwasser and Eldad Regev. A key aim for Hezbollah had been to seize soldiers to use as hostages. An immediate rescue mission was thwarted, with the deaths of five Israeli soldiers. Israel then targeted transport infrastructure and other targets in Lebanon to try to prevent Hezbollah from moving the two hostages. Within days the situation had escalated dramatically and Israel mounted an invasion of southern Lebanon and engaged in widespread fighting with Hezbollah. For four weeks the Israel Defence Force attempted to locate the two men but failed. By the time a ceasefire was declared and the IDF pulled back, 119 Israeli soldiers had been killed and over 1,000 injured. Hezbollah lost between 500–1,000 dead. Civilian casualties were estimated in the thousands. In 2008, the dead bodies of the two hostages were exchanged for the release of over 200 prisoners in Israeli jails.

# Terrorists in their own words

**58.** *Killing Rage* (1997) by Eamon Collins with Mick McGovern. This is a superb autobiography about Collins' life as a member of the IRA in Newry in the 1980s. It stands as perhaps the finest and most insightful autobiography ever written by a terrorist.

**59.** *Mini-manual of the Urban Guerrilla* (1969) by Carlos Marighella. Published shortly before he was killed in a police ambush, this remains one of the most influential terrorism books of the 20th century and is still referred to by contemporary terrorists. The book provides an insightful analysis of the conditions and methods needed to mount a successful terrorist (urban guerrilla) campaign, stressing the importance of winning what came to be called the 'hearts and minds' battle.

**60.** *Knights Under the Prophet's Banner* (2001) by Ayman al-Zawahiri. Part-autobiography, part Al-Qaeda roadmap, no other book describes the group's ideology and strategy in as much detail or with as much insight as this volume.

**61.** *Guerrilla Warfare* (1961) by Che Guevara. This was an attempt by Guevara to distil the key lessons from the Cuban Revolution so that they could be applied in other struggles. Widely read and very influential in the first 20 years after its publication, it was gradually overshadowed by Marighella's *Mini-manual*.

**62.** *The Turner Diaries* (1978) by William Luther Pierce. Sometimes referred to as the bible of the American militia movement, the book is a fictional account of a terrorist campaign. It is famous for pushing the concept of 'leaderless resistance', i.e. that individuals (or small groups) should mount operationally independent campaigns of violence for ideologically similar reasons.

**63.** *Long Walk to Freedom* (1995) by Nelson Mandela. A remarkable and highly detailed autobiography, much of which was originally written while Mandela was in prison. A fascinating account of the life of one of the most important political figures of the past 50 years

**64.** *My Home, My Land: A Narrative of the Palestinian Struggle* (1981) by Abu Iyad with Eric Rouleau. Abu Iyad was a senior member of Fatah and was deeply involved in many of the most notorious terrorist attacks carried out by Palestinian groups in the 1960s and 1970s (including at the Munich Olympics). He provides here a fascinating account of that era.

# Myths about terrorism

**65.** Terrorists are crazy. Most terrorists have a surprisingly normal psychology. The few exceptions tend to be fringe players rather than central figures. Crazy people simply do not make effective terrorists.

66. **Terrorists never win.** Terrorists do win. Between 6–10 per cent of terrorist conflicts will end with the terrorist group triumphant.

67. **Terrorism is a modern problem.** Every generation seems to think that the terrorism of its era is unique and unprecedented. What we call terrorism today has been around for at least 2,000 years, and probably much longer.

68. **Once a terrorist, always a terrorist.** Most terrorists will eventually leave the group and move away from a life of violence. Few released terrorist prisoners re-engage with violence and breaking the law.

69. **Terrorism is the most serious threat facing the world today.** Relatively speaking, very few people are killed by terrorism, even in nations that perceive themselves to be at high risk. In the ten years from 1992 to 2002, 3,500 Americans lost their lives as a result of terrorism (making it the worst ten years ever for Americans in this regard). In comparison, in the same period, over 210,000 Americans were the victims of criminal murder, over 300,000 committed suicide, 420,000 were killed in automobile accidents, 5.4 million died of cancer and nearly 7.5 million died of heart disease.

70. **Terrorists are the same as other criminals.** Terrorists tend to be better educated, more likely to have average or higher IQs, more likely to come from middle or upper class backgrounds, and they are more likely to be psychologically stable compared to other criminals.

71. **Most/all terrorists are Muslim.** Muslim terrorists are very high profile at the moment, but over the past 50 years only a minority of terrorists have come from Muslim backgrounds or been inspired by Islamic-related ideologies. Over 90 per cent of terrorist attacks in the West in the past two decades have been carried out by non-Muslims.

**72.** Terrorist violence is random and indiscriminate. Terrorism is normally the result of a clear decision-making process, with weapons and targets (even civilian ones) carefully selected to obtain specific impacts. The violence is linked to an overall political strategy.

**73.** Harsh retaliation is the best way to respond to terrorism. Harsh counter-measures usually either make the situation worse or else have no long-term positive impact.

**74.** Tackling the root causes of terrorism will quickly resolve a terrorist conflict. Once a terrorist campaign has started, tackling the root causes will probably make little difference in the short- to medium-term. This is a long-term response, not a quick fix.

**75.** You can never negotiate with terrorists. Yes, you can. Some negotiations will produce positive outcomes, many will fail entirely. Almost every state, however, ends up negotiating with terrorists at some stage (including those with an official 'no negotiation' policy).

**76.** Poverty causes terrorism. This is a widely held belief but the evidence for it is much weaker than many realize. Most terrorists come from the middle classes of their societies, and increasing levels of poverty in a society are not linked with an increased risk of terrorism.

# Top movies featuring terrorism

**77.** *The Battle of Algiers* (1966), directed by Gillo Pontecono. A stunningly brilliant film depicting the doomed French effort to retain control in Algeria. Probably the most compelling – and most important – film ever made about terrorism and counter-terrorism.

**78.** *The Life of Brian* (1979), directed by Terry Jones. Famous for its irreverent swipe at organized religion, but just as incisive in its portrayal of terrorist groups, their obsessions, bickering and rivalries. Very clever and profoundly insightful.

**79.** *Flight 93* (2006), directed by Paul Greengrass. By far the best of the films about 9/11, this is a powerfully gripping account of the hijacking of United Airlines flight 93 and the desperate attempt by the passengers and crew to retake control.

**80.** *One Day in September* (1999), directed by Kevin Macdonald. An Oscar-winning documentary about the 1972 Munich Olympics hostage crisis, told from all sides. Tense and compelling.

**81.** *In the Name of the Father* (1993), directed by Jim Sheridan. A powerful film based on the life of Gerry Conlon, who was wrongly convicted of carrying out bombings for the IRA and spent years in jail as a result. A damning indictment of counter-terrorism gone astray.

**82.** *Cry Freedom* (1987), directed by Richard Attenborough. Based on the life and death of anti-apartheid activist, Steve Biko, and the subsequent attempt by a journalist to expose the fact that Biko died as the result of police torture.

**83.** *Four Lions* (2010), directed by Christopher Morris. Another film which uses humour to make incredibly important points. An insightful and surprisingly realistic portrayal of the hapless banality of four British suicide bombers as they prepare to carry out a 'martyrdom operation'.

**84.** *Team America: World Police* (2004), directed by Trey Parker. A brilliant satire on the war on terror. If another film makes the point better than this that counter-terrorism can be even more dangerous than terrorism, I haven't seen it. Not for the easily offended.

**85.** *Che* (2008), directed by Steven Soderbergh. A powerful, if flawed, two-part epic, detailing the highs and lows of the life of Che Guevara. An impressive performance by Benicio del Toro as the central character.

**86.** *The Day of the Jackal* (1973), directed by Fred Zinnemann. The plot has been copied repeatedly but the original still stands apart. Superb tension as Michael Lonsdale's police inspector tries to track down Edward Fox's ruthless assassin before he can kill the French president.

# Terrorists in fiction

**87.** *The Secret Agent* (1908) by Joseph Conrad. Widely regarded as one of the great works of literature of the early 20th century, the bleak plot is nevertheless curiously modern, centred on a police inspector's efforts to track down terrorists in London (and was loosely based on events that occurred in the 1890s). The novel is also notable for being perhaps the first account of a terrorist suicide bomber in fiction.

**88.** *The Cobra Event* (1998) by Richard Preston. Famous for the impact it had on US president Bill Clinton who, after reading it, grew increasingly concerned about the threat of biological terrorism. The book's plot revolves around a terrorist attack on New York City using a lethal virus.

**89.** *Harry's Game* (1975) by Gerald Seymour. Famous for giving us the line 'One man's terrorist is another man's freedom fighter'. The plot centred around an undercover British agent who attempts to infiltrate the IRA. Seymour was a journalist who had covered violence in Northern Ireland and elsewhere.

**90.** *The Day of the Jackal* (1971) by Frederick Forsyth. A superbly taut plot based on a fictional attempt in the 1960s to assassinate President Charles de Gaulle of

France. Notable for the high quality of the research, this was investigative journalist Forsyth's first novel but launched a highly successful writing career.

91. *Black Sunday* (1975) by Thomas Harris. Harris later earned fame as the creator of serial killer Hannibal Lector, but this early novel anticipates both the rise of mass casualty terrorism and the use of suicide tactics in later decades. The plot centres on Palestinian terrorists' efforts to attack the Super Bowl and kill tens of thousands of spectators, including the US president.

# *'What if'* attacks

92. Gunpowder plot, London, 1605. A small group of Roman Catholics planned to destroy the Palace of Westminster during the state opening of Parliament on 5 November 1605, and in the process kill King James I, his elder son, and the members of the House of Lords and the House of Commons, wiping out the British Protestant government. In the aftermath the plotters hoped to incite a Catholic rebellion. The plot came close to succeeding and the explosives were uncovered just 24 hours before the planned detonation. Had the attack succeeded, some form of civil war was likely. The end result would either have been a vehemently anti-Catholic administration or else the restoration of a Catholic monarchy. Either scenario would probably have avoided the English Civil War in 1642, which in turn would probably have meant a very bloody revolution at some point in the 18th or 19th century.

93. Attempt to kill Hitler, Munich, 1939. On 8 November 1939, a bomb intended to kill Adolf Hitler exploded in Munich, killing eight people. The bomb had been planted by Georg Elser in a podium from which Hitler had just spoken. Unlike many later plots, this attempt occurred at a time

when Hitler's death could have had real consequences for the course of the Second World War. In particular, it is possible that the German invasion of the USSR in 1941 may not have occurred. If Nazi Germany had instead focused all its resources on defeating Great Britain, it is possible that the UK might have been knocked out of the war before the USA became involved. Without having to tackle the threat posed by the UK, any subsequent invasion of the USSR would have been much more likely to succeed. Hitler's death at this stage, ironically, could have made an overall Nazi victory in the Second World War much more likely.

**94.** **Hijacking of Air France flight 8969, 1995.** On Christmas Eve 1995, four members of the Armed Islamic Group seized control of Air France flight 8969 while it was on the ground at Algiers' Houari-Boumedienne Airport. Eventually allowed to fly to Marseilles Airport, the hijackers demanded the plane be resupplied with an excessive amount of fuel. It is believed the hijackers intended to detonate the plane over Paris – or possibly to ram it into a major structure in the city. Fearing such an outcome, the plane was stormed by French police at Marseilles and all of the terrorists were killed. Had the Paris plot succeeded, one possible outcome is that 9/11 might never have happened because of increased international recognition that passenger jets could be used as suicide weapons.

**95.** **IRA attack on 10 Downing Street, London, 1991.** On 7 February 1991, the IRA fired three mortars at the British prime minister's residence at 10 Downing Street in London. The prime minister, John Major, was meeting with the Cabinet in the building when the attack occurred. Had anyone been killed – the mortars narrowly missed – it is very likely that the Northern Ireland peace process would have been postponed by at least a decade and possibly longer.

96. **Aum plot to acquire Ebola, Zaire, 1992.** No terrorist group has made as much effort to develop and acquire biological weapons as Aum Shinrikyo. In 1992, after a Japanese tourist died in Zaire (now the Democratic Republic of Congo) from the highly infectious and highly lethal Ebola virus, Aum dispatched a 40-strong team to try to acquire samples. The team spent weeks visiting hospitals in Zaire but failed to acquire the sought-after virus and eventually returned to Japan empty-handed. Had they succeeded, it is certain they would have tried to use Ebola to carry out mass casualty attacks in Japan, in what could have been the most lethal terrorist attacks ever.

97. **IRA plot against Winston Churchill, London, 1921.** On a car journey in London, a police bodyguard spotted an IRA team preparing to assassinate Churchill. The hit squad was evaded, but had Churchill been killed in 1921, the significance would probably have been less about the impact on the Anglo-Irish conflict (though that possibly would have been prolonged), and much more about what would have happened in the 1940s. Would the UK have been able to effectively resist Nazi Germany in 1940–1 without Churchill's inspired leadership?

98. **Attempt to kill Napoleon, Paris, 1800.** On Christmas Eve 1800, an enormous bomb (an 'infernal machine') exploded just behind Napoleon's carriage as he travelled to the opera. The bomb killed or wounded over 50 of his entourage and passers-by, but Napoleon himself was unharmed. Had he been killed, the course of European history would have been very different. Whether Napoleon would have been replaced by another dictator is far from certain, as is the likelihood that any other French leader would have enjoyed the same level of military success in the following ten years. On the plus side for the French, it is also unlikely that there would have been the disastrous invasions of Spain and Russia without Napoleon at the helm.

**99. Iraqi plot to assassinate former US president George H. W. Bush, 1993.** Kuwaiti authorities claimed in 1993 that Iraqi intelligence agents had planned to assassinate the former US president George H. W. Bush when he visited Kuwait that year. The US launched missile strikes against Iraq in retaliation, but had the former president actually been killed, it could have precipitated much more serious action against the Iraqi regime, possibly leading to its removal long before 2003. This potentially could have destabilized the wider region throughout the 1990s and perhaps accelerated the rise of Al-Qaeda and its affiliates. Alternatively, it would have removed the need to invade Iraq in 2003, which would have helped to keep the war on terror focused on Al-Qaeda and key areas in Afghanistan and Pakistan.

**100. Zionist plot to bomb London, 1947**: In early September 1947, French police carried out a series of arrests in connection with a Zionist plot to bomb London from the air. The plan was to drop several home-made bombs and leaflets on London from a chartered plane flown to England from France. The plotters, led by Baruch Korff, had hoped a spectacular operation in London would hasten a British withdrawal from Palestine. If British civilians had been killed in such an attack, however, the government would have been under increased domestic pressure not to withdraw, with potentially very significant consequences for the emergence of Israel as a state.

# Select bibliography

Bakker, E. (2007). *Jihadi terrorists in Europe, their characteristics and the circumstances in which they joined the jihad: an exploratory study* (The Hague: Clingendael Institute).

Bergman, J. (1983). *Vera Zasulich: A Biography* (Stanford, CA: Stanford University Press).

Bjorgo, T. (2005). *Root Causes of Terrorism* (London: Routledge).

Bjorgo, T. and Horgan, J. (2008). *Leaving Terrorism Behind: Individual and Collective Disengagement* (London: Routledge).

Bloom, M. (2006). *Dying to Kill: The allure of suicide terror* (New York: Columbia University Press).

Borum, R. (2004). *Psychology of Terrorism* (Tampa, FL: University of South Florida).

Carr, M. (2011). *The Infernal Machine: An Alternative History of Terrorism* (London: Hurst).

Collins, E. with McGovern, M. (1997). *Killing Rage* (London: Granta Books).

Crenshaw, M. (1981). 'The Causes of Terrorism', *Comparative Politics*, 13(4), pp.379–99.

Cronin, A. (2009). *How Terrorism Ends* (Princeton, NJ: Princeton University Press).

de Cataldo Neuburger, L. and Valentini, T. (1996). *Women and Terrorism* (London: Macmillan).

Dolnik, A. (2007). *Understanding Terrorist Innovation* (London: Routledge).

Drake, C. (1998). *Terrorists' Target Selection* (London: Macmillan).

Fair, C. and Shepherd, B. (2006). 'Who supports terrorism? Evidence from fourteen Muslim countries', *Studies in Conflict and Terrorism*, 29/1, pp.51–74.

Field, A. (2005). *Mainliner Denver: The Bombing of Flight 629* (Boulder, CO: Johnson Books).

Footman, D. (1968). *Red Prelude: A Life of A. I. Zhelyabov* (London: Barrie and Rockliff).

Hoffman, B. (2006). *Inside Terrorism* (New York: Colombia University Press).

Horgan, J. (2005). *The Psychology of Terrorism* (London: Routledge).

Josephus, F. (n.d.). *The Wars of the Jews: or History of the Destruction of Jerusalem* (William Whiston translation), accessed at www.gutenberg.org/ebooks/2850

Kilcullen, D. (2009). *The Accidental Guerrilla* (Oxford: Oxford University Press).

Krueger, A. B. and Maleckova, J. (2002). *Education, poverty, political violence, and terrorism: Is there a causal connection?*, Working Paper No. 9074, National Bureau of Economic Research. Available at http://papers.nber.org/papers/w9074

Mansfield, L. (2006). *His Own Words: A translation of the writings of Dr Ayman al-Zawahiri* (Old Tappan, NJ: TLG Publications).

Pape, R. (2005). *Dying to Win: The Strategic Logic of Suicide Terrorism* (New York: Random House).

Piazza, J. (2006). 'Rooted in Poverty? Terrorism, poor economic development and social cleavages', *Terrorism and Political Violence*, 18/1, pp.159–171.

Rapoport, D. (2004). 'The Four Waves of Modern Terrorism', in A. Kurth Cronin and J. Ludes (eds), *Attacking Terrorism: Elements of a Grand Strategy* (Washington D.C.: Georgetown University Press), pp.46–72.

Reich, W. (1990). *Origins of Terrorism: Psychologies, Ideologies, Theologies, States of Mind* (Cambridge, NY: Woodrow Wilson International Center for Scholars and Cambridge University Press).

Rohner, D. and Frey, B. (2007). 'Blood and ink! The common-interest-game between terrorists and the media.' *Public Choice*, 133, pp.129–145.

Sageman, M. (2004). *Understanding Terrorist Networks* (Philadelphia, PA: University of Pennsylvania Press).

Sanchez-Cuenca, I. (2008). *Revolutionary Dreams and Terrorist Violence in the Developed World: Explaining Country Variation*. Available at http://www.march.es/ceacs/proyectos/dtv/pdf/Revolutionary%20terrorism%20jpr.pdf

Schmid, A. (2011). *The Routledge Handbook of Terrorism Research* (London: Routledge).

Silke, A. (2003). *Terrorists, Victims and Society: Psychological Perspectives on Terrorism and Its Consequences* (Chichester: Wiley).

Silke, A. (2011). *The Psychology of Counter-terrorism* (London: Routledge).

Taylor, M. and Quayle, E. (1994). *Terrorist Lives* (London: Brassey's).

Van Evera, S. (1999). *Causes of War: Power and the Roots of Conflict* (Ithaca, NY: Cornell University Press).

Weimann, G. and Winn, C. (1994). *The Theater of Terror: Mass Media and International Terrorism* (New York: Longman).

Wilkinson, P. (2001). *Terrorism versus Democracy: The Liberal State Response* (London: Frank Cass).

Worthy, W. (1970). 'A real bomber's chilling reasons', *Life*, 68/11 (March 27), p.30.

# Picture credits

The author and publisher would like to give their thanks for permission to use the following images:

The Reign of Terror during the French Revolution, Octobre_1793,_supplice_de_9_emigres

Assassination of Tsar Alexander II, www.heritage-history.com/books/dole/russia/zpage507.gif

Black September terrorist during the Munich Olympics hostage crisis, 1972 © Fairfax Media via Getty Images

Bloody Sunday, Northern Ireland, 1972 © Rex Features/Daily Mail

Timothy McVeigh © Rex Features/Owen/Keystone USA

Samson destroying the main hall of the Philistines, www.teachingcollegeenglish.com/wp-content/uploads/2011/11/samson-illustration-pulling-down-pillars.jpg

Aftermath of sarin attack in Tokyo, 1995 © Rex/Sipa Press

US troops on patrol in Kabul, 2009 © Reuters/Omar Sobhani

Oil pumps silhouetted against the sunset © Shutterstock.com

# Index

ALL THAT MATTERS: TERRORISM